Colossians

Other Founders Study Guide Commentaries

• *Malachi: Founders Study Guide Commentary* – Baruch Maoz
expositional comments on the book of Malachi

• *1 Corinthians: Founders Study Guide Commentary*
– Curtis Vaughan & Thomas D. Lea
expositional comments on the book of 1 Corinthians

• *James: Founders Study Guide Commentary* – Curtis Vaughan
expositional comments on the book of James

• *Ephesians: Founders Study Guide Commentary* – Curtis Vaughan
expositional comments on the book of Ephesians

• *Galatians: Founders Study Guide Commentary* – Curtis Vaughan
expositional comments on the book of Galatians

• *Acts: Founders Study Guide Commentary* – Curtis Vaughan
expositional comments on the book of Acts

• *1,2,3 John: Founders Study Guide Commentary* – Curtis Vaughan
expositional comments on the books of 1 John, 2 John and 3 John

Other Founders Press Titles

• *By His Grace and For His Glory* – Tom Nettles
a historical, theological and practical study of the doctrines of grace in Baptist
life: revised and expanded 20th anniversary edition

• *The Baptism of Disciples Alone* – Fred Malone
sets out to prove that the Bible authorizes only credobaptism, the baptism
of disciples alone

• *Dear Timothy* – Edited by Tom Ascol
collection of writings from seasoned pastors contains over 480 years of
combined ministry experience for old and new pastors alike

• *Truth & Grace Memory Books (#1, #2, & #3)* — Edited by Tom Ascol
a solid plan for children's Bible study, Scripture memory,
catechetical instruction and exposure to great hymns

FOUNDERS STUDY GUIDE COMMENTARY

Colossians
Christ All-Sufficient

Baruch Maoz

Founders Press
Cape Coral, Florida

Published by
Founders Press

P.O. Box 150931 • Cape Coral, FL 33915
Phone (239) 772–1400 • Fax: (239) 772–1140
Electronic Mail: founders@founders.org or
Website: http://www.founders.org

©2014, 2018 Baruch Maoz

Printed in the United States of America

ISBN: 978–1–943539–10–9

Scripture quotations marked NASB are from the NEW AMERICAN STANDARD BIBLE®. © The Lockman Foundation 1960, 1962, 1963, 1968, 1971, 1972, 1973, 1975, 1977, 1995. Used by permission.

Scripture quotations marked ESV are from THE ENGLISH STANDARD VERSION. ©2001 by Crossway Bibles, a division of Good News Publishers.

Dedication

Dedicated to Avital, Shlomit and Tamar,
who have brought me much joy
and challenged me often
to be more of what I ought to be in Christ
and less of what I am.

Contents

Preface

As in my previous devotional commentaries, I offer at the beginning of each chapter my translation of Colossians. Unless indicated otherwise, the translations of other Scriptures are mine as well. I do not presume to provide a proper literary rendering of the Greek. My object is to try to give a sense of the text that more traditional translations cannot offer because of grammatical and literary expectations they are obliged to meet.

Paul's thoughts are complicated. His sentences are often long as history (see, for example, Colossians 1:5-21). His thoughts are closely interwoven, with one idea leading to another while enlarging on earlier thoughts. Translations, especially modern translations, tend to abbreviate sentences and force texts into literary conventions. As a result, they must sometimes obscure the connection between ideas.

In effort to draw readers closer to the text and enable them to discover more of its nuances, I've provided a somewhat more literal, decidedly less literary rendition of the New Testament text. Sometimes my translation transgresses modern grammatical rules or is stilted in terms of flow. This is the inevitable product of an effort to render the text in a more literal fashion. I am trying to convey the actual text, thereby allowing readers to measure my comments by the text and to determine the meaning for themselves.

In this context, there are two distinctions made in what follows and to which I wish to draw your attention. First, Paul draws a distinction between faith as an attitude of heart and the Faith, which refers to the content of what is believed. I have sought to draw the same distinction. Second, and no less important, it seems to me that Paul draws a distinction between law in general and the Law given to Israel at Sinai. At least in most cases (especially in his letters to the Romans and to the Galatians), he speaks of law in general without the definite article and of the Law of Moses by employing it. Again, assuming I am right, I have sought to make the same distinction.

Many commentaries, far better than this one, tend to focus on the trees of Paul's wording rather than on the forest of his broader intentions. Some of my earlier books suffer from the same shortcoming. I am referring to the tendency to deal with texts sentence by sentence, paragraph by paragraph, often with little reference to the main theme or themes of the composition as a whole. This is especialy evident when looking at the "practical" sections of Paul's letters. The biblical message was delivered as an entire text, not isolated passages, let alone isolated verses, and in response to specific situations. The principles enunciated and the practices called for are consistent with the issues raised and the situations addressed. I have endevored to draw the reader's attention to this relationship in the course of my comments, with the goal of encouraging readers to constantly view the book as a whole. This is not a criticim of those others works; it is merely an attempt to explain the logic of the approach adopted in this work. If some do not see the forest for the trees, I am aware of the equal truth that there cannot be a forest without trees. Both appraoches are needed.

This is not an academic commentary. It is not meant to stand alongside those excellent works of careful exegesis scholars produce and from which my effort at understanding Paul has benefited so much. What I have learned from them is, I hope, reflected in what follows. The goal set for this work is to explain the text in a devotional, nontechnical manner that will assist readers in applying the Scriptures to their lives. It is also meant to encourage reading biblical books as a unified whole, rather than according to the piecemeal approach we often adopt in our preaching and devotions.

My longing in this series is to encourage a love of God's Word, born out of a vivid understanding of the text and an affectionate comprehension of its relevancy. I long to help readers fall in love with Jesus and grow in loving obedience to him. I long to draw you, dear reader, closer to God; provide you with a broad, practical understanding of the gospel; help you realize you need nothing beyond Christ, and that you *do* need him. To that end, I have tried to write in a way that is easy to follow and yet challenging and helpful.

If I manage to discomfort you through the truths of this amazing letter, encourage you toward a more conscious dependency on Christ, or help you understand something more of the power of the gospel; if the Spirit of Jesus works in your life, transforming these words from mere verbiage into God's power to save, bless and sanctify, I will have achieved my desire.

May God bless you as you read.

Baruch Maoz
Mazkeret Batya, Israel
June 2017

Introduction

TO THE BOOK OF COLOSSIANS

Paul

Paul of Tarsus, the author of this letter to the church in Colossae, was born and initially educated in what appears to have been a rather wealthy Jewish family near Antioch of Syria, in the Roman province of Cilicia. (This area is now eastern Turkey. There was another Antioch, in Pisidia, which was part of the province of Asia in what is now central western Turkey.) He "conformed to the strictest sect [of Judaism], living as a Pharisee" (Acts 26:5), which is why he traveled to Jerusalem to study under Rabbi Gamaliel, one of the most influential rabbis in Jewish history. There he was "taught according to the perfect manner of the law of the fathers and was zealous toward God" (Acts 22:3; see also Philippians 3:2), so much so that he took an active part in the initial attempts to stamp out faith in Jesus, the Christ, and "persecuted the followers of this way unto death, arresting both men and women and throwing them into prison" (Acts 22:4).

The apostle had all the credentials necessary for a thorough understanding of the Jewish Faith. He knew the Torah, the Jewish tradition, and the distinct interpretations of both as formulated by the Pharisees, the forefathers of modern Judaism.

When faith in Jesus first emerged within the Jewish nation, Paul sought authorization from the High Priests to extinguish it among adherents as far away as Damascus (Acts 9:1–2). On his way there he was stopped in his tracks by the living Jesus, converted to the Faith he sought to destroy, and baptized shortly after arriving in the city (Acts 9:3–18).

Following some three years of contemplation in the wilderness (Galatians 1:15–18), Paul returned to Damascus, proclaimed the Faith, and then was forced to flee for his life (Acts 9:19–25). When he arrived in Jerusalem, the church there viewed him as troublesome and sent him home (Acts 9:26–31). Obviously, although called, he was not yet mature enough in the Faith to embark onto his mission. That would require some more years of spiritual and personal growth and a confirmation of his call by the Holy Spirit through the church.

Many years later, he was called to work alongside Barnabas in Syrian Antioch (Acts 11:26) and embarked with him, as his junior, onto what turned out to be his first missionary journey (Acts 13:1–14:27). When a controversy arose in the church regarding the place of the ritual law and of Jewish tradition in the Christian life (Galatians 2:11–21), the church sent him and Barnabas to have the matter discussed and determined by the apostles and elders of the church in Jerusalem (Acts 15:1–2). This ocurred some 14-17 years after his conversion (Galatians 1:18, 2:1) There in Jerusalem, Paul, the former student of the famously strict Pharisaic Rabbi Gamliel, insisted everything the Torah and tradition promised but could not deliver was to be found in Christ, and that Christian commitment was now to be directed exclusively toward Jesus, the Christ, rather than to the Torah or Jewish tradition. His view won the day.

In all, Paul conducted what turned out to be three missionary tours, the first in the company of Barnabas and during which he emerged as the leader among the two. The other two on his own (Acts 15:1–18:18; 18:19–21:7). Each tour reached an ever-broader area of the Roman world and Paul laid out plans to travel with the gospel as far as Spain (Romans 15:24, 28). He might had gone still farther if God in His providence had not chosen otherwise. The apostle aspired to conquer the world for Jesus and to bring all nations under Christ's sway. He passionately believed God was not only the God of the Jews but also of the Gentiles.

Most of the time Paul itinerated, spending only a few weeks in any one location. But he chose to stay in Corinth (Greece) and Ephesus (what is now western Turkey) for extended periods (Acts 18:1–11; 19:1–10). In the course of his tours, he wrote 1 and 2 Thessalonians, Galatians, the two letters to the Corinthians, and Romans. At the end of each of the first two tours, he returned to Antioch and reported to the church there (Acts 14:24–28; 18:18–24). The third tour ended in Jerusalem (Acts 21:1–15).

While in Jerusalem, he was arrested after being falsely charged with desecrating the temple and almost lynched by an angry mob (Acts 21:27–

36). He remained for two years under arrest in Caesarea (Acts 23:12–26:32) and then was shipped, at his request, to be tried before Nero, the Roman Caesar. In Rome, he awaited imperial decision under detention for another two years (Acts 28:16–31) before being released. Meanwhile, he wrote Ephesians (probably a circular letter to churches; the copy we have was delivered to the church in Ephesus), Colossians, Philemon, and Philippians.

Upon release, Paul traveled to Ephesus and Crete (1 Timothy 1:3; Titus 1:5), among other places (2 Timothy 4:13, 20), and wrote his final letters to Timothy and Titus. He was executed in Rome somewhere around AD 64. This would date Paul's letter to the Colossians somewhere around AD 62–63. The exact dates of the apostle's career are a matter of scholarly debate into which we need not enter. The dates quoted here are approximate. What is impressive is how short Paul's career turned out to be and what an impact it had on the world. Paul was converted somewhere around 33 AD and set out on his first missionary journey at or after 46 AD, at least 14 years later. That indicates a maximum of 18 years of extremely productive ministry that, literally, changed the course of history. Few have ever acheived so much in so short a time.

A central theme in Paul's preaching and writing was the completeness and sufficiency of Christ's achievements. These, the apostle insisted, were the grounds of saving and sanctifying grace. They were also the grounds for Christian fellowship. Paul could not imagine a salvation that did not include sanctification; that is to say, the spiritual and moral transformation of individuals, communities, and nations.

Nor could he imagine such a transformation apart from grace. Grace, in Paul's view, is God in action; it pointed both to God's independence of, and love for, man. It secured the purposes of God for the world and was, therefore, the impetus behind both the doctrine of the church and the doctrine of last things (also known by the term eschatology). Grace was to find practical expression in the lives of those who experienced salvation: they were to conduct moral lives, their morality motivated, shaped, and directed by a loving fear of God and an appreciation of His kindness. That, in Paul's mind, was a fundamental expression of true spirituality.

Christians were to proclaim the gospel by their conduct, pointing to the sufficiency of grace by pointing to the sufficiency of Christ's achievements in all walks of life. Among other ways, this was to be shown by the fact that distinctions between people were rendered immaterial: social standing and gender (both major issues in the Roman world), nationality (a major issue to Jewish minds), culture (an important aspect of Greek and Roman thinking) — none of these could form the basis for anything of value before God. Nor should they be allowed to separate Christians. It did not matter if you were a slave or a freeman, a man or a woman, a Jew or a Gentile; only grace made a difference, and it made all the difference in the world.

That is why Paul insisted on unity between Jews and Gentiles and of others in the church. Such unity pointed to Christ, demonstrated the power of the gospel, taught men and women to rely on no one but Christ, assured them of God's ultimate victory on the grounds of Christ's life, death, and resurrection, and provided them with a vivid, practical view of Christ's wondrous glory.

Paul did not think of church life extemporaneously. Nor did he look for the most "effective" way to promote his message. While no one in history could claim more evangelistic zeal than Paul, his concept of church life was not focused on evangelism but on God, as He is known in Christ, and on the nature of the gospel. He understood the church to be a visible manifestation of the gospel and was guided by the essential principles of that gospel. There was nothing *ad hoc*, nothing motivated by practicality in his understanding of the required conduct of the church. He lived out his theology and expected the churches he founded to live in the same way. Was he wrong, or is there something we need to learn with regard to church practice today?

Colossae

Colossae was situated in what was then known as Phrygian territory, an area colonized for hundreds of years by Greek settlers, now known as mid-western Turkey and then the Roman province of Asia (Acts 16:6; 19:10, 26). The culture was a brew of mystical, notoriously excitable Phrygian practices and thoughtful, almost rationalistic Greek intellectual guesses at the nature of reality, mixed with the belief in many gods.

The city had known much better days. Hierapolis and Laodicea were close by, but Colossae's position had formerly given it prominence. It was situated at the junction of the Lycus River near a mountain pass and two important tributaries, perched above a fertile valley through which one could travel north east to the great city of Smyrna, westward and downriver to the port of bustling Miletus, or west to the prestigious port of Ephesus. Colossae had served as an important depot on the way from the Euphrates River via Persia, all the way to the country now known as India. The city was also known for its excellent climate and its famous textile and dyeing industry.

The Jewish community in the city was largely the product of Antiochus the Great's deportation of two thousand Jewish families from Babylon to the area. However, some Israelites settled in there as far back as the Assyrian dispersion of the ten tribes, just under eight hundred years earlier. The Babylonian Talmudic Tractate, Sabbath (147, b), compiled some 100 to 150 years later, complained that the pleasures of Phrygia caused many of the Jewish families to assimilate, turning their backs on Jewish customs. Some of these families would have resided in Colossae. In his book *Saint Paul's Epistles to the Colossians and Philemon*, John Lightfoot mentioned that in AD 62 there was a confiscation of money, collected by the Jews of the area, for the temple in Jerusalem, the sum of which indicates a population of some eleven thousand adults.[1] Acts 2:10 makes mention of Phrygians among those who came to worship in Jerusalem, some of whom were likely to have been from Colossae.

Xerxes and Cyrus the Younger stopped here in 481 and 401 BC respectively on their way to invade Greece. Anyone of any prominence who traveled in the area inevitably passed through or near Colossae at some time: tribunes with their courtiers, soldiers, senators on the way to or from the East, merchants from the East and the West burdened with their wares and strange religions, the sumptuous and the ill to visit the local hot springs, rabbis, market philosophers and mystic visionaries who peddled their theories. The city had throbbed with confident expectation of even better days.

Those better days never came. Instead, following an earthquake in AD 17 (followed by another in AD 60), Colossae became a municipal has-been, its economy in decline and its population despondent, with all the social and psychological effects of such circumstances. The city lost its vigor. The inhabitants sank into the petty sullenness that so often characterizes backwater townships void of the exhilaration of expectation and achievement, the Colossians became bored, disenchanted busybodies, engrossed in petty minutia. They lived on the shreds of the past rather than thriving on hopes for the future. There did not seem to be a future. The city's slow decline continued until, by AD 400, only ruins remained.

---

[1] John Barber Lightfoot, *Saint Paul's Epistles to the Colossians and Philemon* (Grand Rapids, MI: Zondervan, 1974), 20.

When Paul composed this letter, he had not visited Colossae (Colossians 1:4, 9, 23; 2:1), although he may or may not have gone through the city in the course of previous travels. The church seems to have been founded by Epaphras (Colossians 1:7-8; not to be confused with Epaphroditus mentioned in the letter to the Philippians. See also Philemon v. 23), a resident of the city (Colossians 4:12). The church was founded sometime in the course of Paul's second missionary journey, during which he spent two to three years in nearby Ephesus (AD 54-57; see Acts 20:31). This might help explain Luke's statement that "all they which dwelt in Asia heard the word of the Lord Jesus, both Jews and Greeks" (Acts 19:10).

Philemon was a prominent believer in the city (Philemon v. 1). He hosted a church in his home (Philemon v. 2) while another was apparently hosted by Nympha (Colossians 4:15). Onesimus (Philemon 10-16; Colossians 4:3, 10, 18), a runaway slave from Philemon's household, had somehow come into contact with Paul during the latter's first confinement to Rome, was converted through the apostle's testimony, and was sent back to Philemon, not only as a slave returning to his owner, but as a brother in Christ. Apparently Philemon was a wealthy person.

Paul's letter to the Colossians is one of the four so-called Prison Letters (the other three are the letters to the Philippians, Philemon, and the Ephesians), all composed while Paul was under guard in Rome sometime near AD 61, no more than six years after the church in Colossae was founded, perhaps less.

The letter to the Colossians was brought to Colossae by Tychicus (4:7-9), who traveled with Onesimus and therefore also carried the letter to Philemon. It was to be shared with the church in Laodicea (4:16), which also received a letter and was to share it with the church in Colossae (4:16).

Paul's letter to the Colossians contains many unique terms (*hapaxlegomena*)—thirty-four to be exact—most of which are in what is probably a hymn quoted in Colossians 1:15-20, and in the apostle's response to false teachers in 2:8-23. Apparently the apostle adopted terms used by the false teachers as a means to demonstrate that the valid aspirations those teachers purported to address are satisfied in Christ.

There are extensive similarities between Paul's language and the arguments of the letters to the Colossians and to the Ephesians. The style and many phrases used are identical. This is a significant factor when discussing issues of authorship. To deny that the same author is responsible for both letters is to fly in the face of the evidence. The theology of the letter to the Colossians is identical with that in Paul's other letters, with distinct emphases dictated by the specifics of reality in Colossae. Paul always insisted on the sufficiency of Christ's accomplishments on behalf of the redeemed.

Like most in his day, Paul used lengthy, complicated sentences, long enough to make an asthmatic run out of breath. The temptation to shorten these in the course of translation is great, but to do so is to lose something of the close connection between the apostle's various statements. For this reason, I have chosen in most cases to render Paul's long—sometimes very long—sentences intact.

Influences

Colossae's position, on a busy thoroughfare between East and West, exposed the city to the best and the worst of Roman-era cultures, as did the makeup of its population. The worship of the Phrygian goddess Cybele was accompanied by frenzied, orgiastic celebrations in which devoted adherents were said to gain access to hidden knowledge of the future. What scholars now describe as a "proto-Gnosticism," probably imported from the East, had begun to influence people's thinking. Assertive mysticism offered the Colossians an illusion of the importance their city had begun to lose: access to the hidden mysteries of the universe, a knowledge unreached by others either because it was not granted or they did not do what was necessary to achieve it. The Christian community in Colossae was not immune.

H. C. G. Moule put it well in his book *Colossian and Philemon Studies* when he said there were those in Colossae to whom "Christ was much, but not enough."[2] The heretics did not deny the validity of their fellow believers' experiences: Jesus saved all Christians and granted them forgiveness of sins. But the Colossian believers were being invited to a purportedly higher spiritual reality that exceeded mere faith and forgiveness: they could have a fuller vision of God, could better comprehend His grandeur, and could achieve a kind of perfection and have direct contact with heavenly beings. In short, they could become super-spiritual. Why, then, settle for less?

[2] H. C. G. Moule, *Colossian and Philemon Studies* (Fort Washington, PA: Christian Literature Crusade, 1932, reprint 1975), 115

The false teachers in Colossae did not understand that the whole of their salvation was in Jesus, that there is no justification for seeking anything beyond Him. Paul enlisted their terminology and turned it around to point to Jesus. This explains his repeated emphasis on terms such as *body* and *flesh, fullness, full, thorough,* and *complete,* as well as his references to *light,* and *knowledge.*

From what Paul said in his letter to the Colossians, we learn that the false teachers claimed to have the means to gain spiritual knowledge, wisdom, and power (1:9–11) and to experience unique access to "the inheritance of the consecrated ones in light" (1:12) through which believers could achieve a higher spirituality and escape "the domain of darkness" (1:13).

The heretics further claimed to be able to contact the *pleroma* (fullness, 1:20), a descending graduation of deities (1:19; 2:9, 18) connecting heaven and earth. Contact with these was said to enable a person to escape the confines of earthly and bodily existence, to access mysteries (1:24, 26–27; 2:2), and to obtain "all the treasures of wisdom and knowledge" (2:3).

Just as the ultimate God was at the top of the ladder of emanations, so the ultimate good was thought to be at the top of the ladder of spiritual enlightenment. Just as the demiurge, the crassest, lowest of divine emanations, was said to have created the material world, so the crassest of Christians lived in touch with the world. Fullness of spirituality was to be achieved by ascending the ladder until the Ultimate was achieved. Some in Colossae believed they had access to angelic patrons who would guide them in the path of enlightenment. Mind you, these heavenly patrons were not to be confused with almighty God; they were of a lower level. But fuller, truer knowledge of God was to be had through them, and through them alone. Spirituality, like the Godhead, was a matter of degrees.

Does this sound familiar? The same promise has been pandered since time began: "You will be like God." "To be such, your eyes need to be opened, and for that to happen you need to reach out beyond the confines of mundane spirituality to the Ultimate. True, few achieve this goal, but you're special. You can do it. Yes, you can."

Some form of what was probably a highly syncretic form of Judaism also had made an impact, resulting in a fascinating list of legalistic 'dos' and 'do nots' including circumcision, practices of self-abasement (including strict prohibitions, see 2:21), and the observance of special days (2:16–18). These easily combined with the various other influences because, contrary to its present reputation, Judaism has always been a highly syncretic religion that imbibed elements from Babylonian, Persian, Greek, Gnostic, and Roman religions.

The proponents of this distorted view of the gospel insisted there were many things truly spiritual Christians shouldn't do and others they should, many of which had to do with worship, how one related to the spiritual and physical world, or what one ate or drank or allowed himself to handle.

Every one of these impositions became a badge of honor, evidence of increased spiritual achievement. The Colossian heretics were devout, serious-minded individuals, willing to forgo earthly pleasures for what they believed to be the gospel. They were intent on spiritual advancement. To that end they developed a series of doctrinal test-terms. The faithful considered themselves to be spiritual elites. Such presumptions always tend to promote arrogance: "I thank you, Lord, that I am not like those others. I am seriously spiritual. I don't do what many Christians do, and I do what they don't. I read the right books, worship in the right congregation, baptize in the correct fashion, and enjoy those things that are conducive to my spirituality. I'm sure you are as pleased with me as I am with myself. Of course, I willingly admit such knowledge is a gift of grace—that's part of my theology—but I have grace, which probably means that, in some mysterious way, I am better than others although my theology asserts the opposite." Those who lacked what these Christians claimed to have belonged to a lower class, however sincere their faith. They were brethren of a lesser sort. Purporting to achieve a higher wisdom and to walk the path to higher spirituality led to pride and therefore to disrupted personal relations (3:1–4:1). Once again, there are modern parallels.

Paul knew better. He insisted in this letter that Christ came in the flesh, that the fullness of the godhead dwells in Him, and that the fullness of spiritual blessing is to be found in Him and in Him alone. Paul knew Christ is all in all, a fully sufficient Savior. He also knew that any obscuring of this truth reflected on the glory of Christ and the sufficiency of His accomplishments. That is why he so firmly opposed the false teaching and sought to rectify its impact. Whatever might have been the intentions of such promoters of higher spirituality; their view of the Faith made light of Christ and offered but a clouded view of His glory. To quote Moule again, who wrote with prophetic insight:

The new voices at Colossae would have many things to discourse upon; and among these many things would be Jesus Christ. But he would not be the magnetic Centre of their discourses. They would not gravitate to Him, and be as if they could never have done with setting forth his holy greatness, and his vital necessity, and his "all-sufficiency in all things." His dying love would not set the speakers' hearts and words on fire, nor would they dilate upon his rising power, and the double blessing of His presence, for his disciples upon the Throne, and His disciples in the heart. The wonder of His incarnation would be little spoken of, and the solemn joy of the hope of His Return as little. The favorite topics of conversation and of preaching would be of a very different kind. Circumcisions, a calendar of obligatory holidays, a code of ceremonial abstinence, a philosophy of unseen powers, and secret ways and rules for approach to them in adoration; these would be the congenial and really characteristic themes of this "other gospel."

Now this, as we know, (thanks under God to our Colossian Epistle among other oracles of the Truth), is exactly unlike the authentic gospel. What is the gospel of the New Testament, or rather of the whole Scriptures, as the New Testament unfolds the hidden glories of the Old? It is not this thing, or that, and the other; it is our Lord Jesus Christ. It is "the proclamation of Jesus Christ." ...

No surer test, according to the Holy Scriptures, can be applied to anything claiming to be Christian that this: Where does it put Jesus Christ. Is He something in it, or is He all? Is He the Sun of the true solar system, so that every planet gets its place and its light from Him? Or is He at best a sort Ptolomaic sun, rolling together with other luminaries around an earthly centre—whether that centre take the form of an observance, a constitution, or a philosophy?[3]

Such theories are often devised with the best intentions in an effort to promote spirituality. But they result in a form of pride that is all the more difficult to uproot—or even detect—precisely because they are disguised as a form of a thoroughgoing spirituality. To the extent that we are like the Colossians (and I suspect there is a Colossian lurking in every one of us), Paul's letter to the church in Colossae is a useful antidote. He carefully crafted it to serve as such, and the Holy Spirit guided him.

---

[3] H. C. G. Moule, *Colossian and Philemon Studies*, 13–15.

Let's Summarize

- Paul wrote this letter around the same time he wrote to the Ephesians and to Philemon, while under detention in Rome. He was equipped by education, experience, and calling to address the issues raised.

- Paul's desire was to bring the world under the rule of Christ, to have all mankind appreciate the wonder of Jesus' saving, sanctifying accomplishments.

- The Christians in Colossae were being invited to aspire to a higher spiritual level than they had upon conversion. This higher level had to do with a mixture of mystical and Jewish elements. Paul opposed the idea that there is anything to be had from God beyond what is provided in Christ. He believed grace, not human endeavor or achievement, is the basis of spirituality and of church unity.

- Paul was a thoughtful man who understood that church life should be expressive of the principles of the gospel.

Let's Pray

Great God of glory and of grace,

the Father of our Lord Jesus, the Christ,

Lord of all life and salvation,

we are humbled and challenged by Paul's example and desire

to follow him as he followed Christ the Savior.

We ask for grace to be what we ought to be,

relying fully on Jesus,

subjecting all our efforts to His majesty and goodness.

Teach us to lead lives consistent with the gospel,

we ask in Jesus' name, amen.

QUESTIONS FOR DISCUSSION AND STUDY

1. What do you think were the reasons for Paul's devotion to Christ? Do you share those reasons? Do they impact you as they impacted him?

2. Expand from Scripture on the connection between the experience of salvation and a moral life. Which precedes which and why? Why is the gospel necessary? What does the gospel have to do with morality?

3. How does the essence of the gospel determine what the life of a church should be? To what extent does your church implement Paul's concept of Christ and of the gospel?

4. How does pride contradict a biblical view of the church and how is it to be countered?

CHAPTER 1

Opening Words
(COLOSSIANS 1:1–8)

1 Paul, an apostle of the Christ Jesus by the will of God, and Timothy the brother, 2 to the consecrated and faithful brothers in Colossae: grace to you and peace from God our Father.

3 As we pray, we always give thanks for you to God, the Father of our Lord Jesus the Christ, 4 having heard of your faith in the Christ Jesus and the love you have for all the consecrated ones 5 because of the hope stored for you in the heavens, of which hope you heard earlier through the truthful word of the gospel 6 which is coming to you as it also does in all the world. It is bearing fruit and growing, as it also does among you from the day you heard and fully and truly experienced the grace of God, 7 as you learned from Epaphras our beloved fellow-slave who is a faithful servant of Christ for your sake, 8 who also described to us your sincere (or, hearty) love.

Who wrote the letter? How we relate to what we read is determined to a large extent by the answer to that question. A brief reminder on a napkin composed by the late president of the United States, John F. Kennedy, is more valuable by far, and its contents the valid object of more attention, than a carefully crafted letter by Mr. Nobody in Particular. Paul was not his own messenger. God sent him; Paul merely obeyed. God is the ultimate the author of this letter.

Could Paul have done otherwise than undertake his mission? Of course not. The God who commanded the light to shine out of darkness, who commanded nothingness to become existence, ordered Paul: "Get up and go into the city, and you will be told what you must do" (Acts 9:6). As Hannaniah put it, "You will be his witness to all the people of what you have seen and heard. And now, what are you waiting for? Get up, be baptized and wash your sins away, calling on His name" (Acts 22:15–16). "So then," Paul said, "I was not disobedient to the vision from heaven" (Acts 26:19). He wrote to the Colossians as a messenger, appointed "by the will of God."

In other words, Paul's message was not his own. He was "an apostle of the Christ," whom he identified as Jesus. Paul's message had primarily to do with the Christ, which is probably why Paul added the definite article and at times mentioned Jesus' title before his name, an order found only in the apostle's writings. Paul's words bore authority because he was Christ's representative. Unlike many purported messengers who focus on health and wealth, the Law, Jewish roots, an experience of the Spirit, the gifts, Calvinism, or eschatology, Christ constitutes the main burden of Paul's message. He was sent to promote Jesus, no one and nothing else. He spoke and wrote nothing but what he had been commissioned to speak and write, and his words were to be heard and heeded.

Paul did not write alone. The letter to the Colossians came from him and from "Timothy the brother." Paul was not inclined to pull rank for a display of honor. When necessary, he did not hesitate to do so, but he also considered it his duty to mentor others, to train and promote them in the ways of the Lord. He did not hesitate to treat Timothy as an equal. Timothy is here described as a brother, Paul's brother, and brother to the Colossians. As such, Timothy wrote with Paul out of concern for the welfare of the Colossian Christians and for the glory of God, on equal par with Paul.

The Colossians were dear to God. They were "the consecrated ones." They had been set aside for Him by virtue of creation, through which mankind belongs to Him, and by the life, sacrifice, and resurrection of Christ and the giving of the Spirit, through which the redeemed are His.

The Colossian Christians had been dedicated by God to Himself. Consecration is not a higher level of spirituality achieved by human means, as the false teachers in Colossae taught. All such human effort is the product of a divine initiative: He consecrates and man responds by devoting himself to God. Every spiritual blessing and every advancement in spiritual life that Christians enjoy are gifts from God in Christ.

Christians should live in the light of this truth. We should look on life as the framework in which we have been consecrated to the service of God.

The Colossians served because they were not only "consecrated," they were also "faithful brothers." They lived as they ought to have lived. It is worth noting, as other commentaries in this series have done, that both the Hebrew and the Greek language view faith and faithfulness as two sides of the same coin. None but those who have faith can be faithful; none can be faithful without faith; all who have faith are inevitably faithful, however much they fail.

These faithful, consecrated ones to which Paul wrote were not figures in a storybook. They were real people who lived in a real place, in this case, "in Colossae." Colossae was the context in which they lived out their life in Christ, but they were to do so more like those who are in Christ than like the others who lived in the city. Their life in Christ was the determining factor, which at times meant they were obliged to resist local influences to be "faithful."

Faithfulness, among other things, meant that the Colossians were to remain true to the faith they had learned from Epaphras. This was the purpose for which Paul penned this letter. He was anxious to encourage them to continue to trust in Jesus and in His accomplishments rather than supplementing what Jesus had done.

"Grace to you and peace from God our Father." Paul enlisted the familiar traditional greeting of his time, transforming it from mere lip service or a literary convention ("Dear so and so, ... Respectfully yours") into a distinctly Christian greeting. Everything the gospel touches is transformed. Cultures are valid expressions of life experienced in community, and when addressed by the gospel, they are changed as lives are changed. Mere words become intentional, full of meaning.

"As we pray, we always give thanks for you to God, the Father of our Lord Jesus the Christ, having heard of your faith in the Christ Jesus and the love you have for all the consecrated ones." Paul assumed the Colossians would take it for granted that he prayed. Prayer is as natural and as commonplace to Christians as breathing. When Paul prayed, he had reason to thank God for the Colossian Christians. The text does not clearly state if the reason of his gratitude was the fact that they believed, that they loved all the consecrated ones, or both (which is most likely), but think about it: Why would the apostle thank God for the Colossians' faith or their love unless God was their effective cause? Paul attributed to God what we might be inclined to attribute to the Colossians.

It is not that God permitted the Colossians to believe or to love (God is glorious energy; He is never passive). It was not that He helped or enabled them to do so. Whatever the reason for Paul's thanksgiving, it was something for which God deserved to be thanked because He was the one who did it. Whatever part the Colossians played in believing and loving, the ultimate determining factor was God, not the Colossians. God's grace moved the Colossians to respond as they ought. That is why the apostle thanked God for what the Colossians did. This is the Paul's first denigration in this letter of human effort. Grace removes all grounds for human boasting, all confidence in human abilities.

Paul knew God as only a Christian can know Him, as "the Father of our Lord Jesus the Christ." Whatever else the title "Father" represents, it certainly represents a relationship identified by two main features. First, that in some way the Father is the origin of the Christ. This is an indication of Christ's deity, strengthened by yet another title Paul accorded Jesus in this passage: "Lord." Christ is divine. He is the Son of the Father and partakes of the same nature with the Father, just as a son partakes of his father's human nature. God is the Creator of the world in which we live. But He is the Father of the Lord Jesus.

Second, Christ is the object of the Father's affection. He is the "beloved," not because of anything he has done, but by necessity, by nature, by virtue of who both He and the Father are. The Father loves the Son as fathers inevitably, naturally, necessarily love their sons, only infinitely more so. The Father and the Son, two of the three glorious persons of the Trinity, love one another. They are a happy fellowship of holy, eternally unconditional affection.

The beloved one is also Lord. In this context, the title (*kurios* in Greek) indicates rule, sovereignty, mastery, power, and authority. Of course, the title was also used in those days much as we would use the term *Mister*. But Christ is not merely a Mister. Being God, He is Lord in the fullest sense of the term. He rules the universe. He rules history. He rules mankind and, in a particular, saving way, He rules those who put their trust in Him for salvation. He is the Master of their destiny, the Ruler of their lives, the faithful Preserver of their souls. His will is their law. His commandment is their duty. *Lord* implies kingship.

That is why Paul made sure to describe Christ as "our Lord." Jesus is Lord over a particular people, whose boast is in Him and whose allegiance is given to Him. Lordship is never abstract, and Christ's lordship is not contingent on man's agreement. His mastership is not derived. No one makes Him Lord; He is such because He is what He is, and modern evangelical parlance, which speaks of "making Jesus Lord of our lives," is less than biblical. Jesus rules because it is in the nature of His divine being. He extends His saving rule over whomever He wishes, and no one can limit His powers.

Conversion is ultimately an act of Christ, laying hold of rebels and changing the direction of their wills, begetting them anew by the power of his Spirit, enlightening their eyes, moving their hearts, convincing them of sin, driving them to repentance, granting them forgiveness, blessing them with assurance, motivating them to holiness, and transforming them still further, ever further, until they are glorified and once again bear the image of the God who created and redeemed them. Salvation is an act of God, an act of "our Lord Jesus the Christ."

This Lord, this Christ, so strong to save, is none other but Jesus. It is amazing how much theology Paul packed into these few words. Jesus is the name of a man, born of a woman, who has a birthday, who ate and slept, coughed and perspired, laughed and wept as He walked on earth. He had a real body, a distinct voice, and a number of brothers and sisters. His birth was real. His pain was real. His death was real. His resurrection was as real as anything else that could be said of Him.

Note, it is not that Jesus was a man and is no longer such. He was not a man who achieved deification, nor can deity be earned or otherwise made one's possession. He did not shed His human name when He rose. Enthroned at the right hand of God, He is still called Jesus. He was God at the same time that He was man, and continues to be man at the same time He is God. He rose bodily, as the man Christ Jesus, and ascended to sit at the right hand of God. He is human today, just as He is God, and He is Jesus today, just as He is Lord and Christ.

We concluded that Paul thanked God for one of two reasons, or (most likely) for both:

1. "Having heard of your faith in the Christ Jesus" and

2. Having heard "the love you have for all the consecrated ones."

We've also noted that God was the author of the Colossians' faith. Now we learn that their faith was directed toward "the Christ Jesus." Of course, faith of the saving kind should be directed toward God, because only God saves. So here we have another indication of the deity of Christ. What does it mean to have faith in Him for salvation? It means to trust

Him, to confidently believe that He is capable of saving, and to entrust Him with our eternal destiny.

Could we trust anyone but God with such a treasure? Is Jesus worthy of such trust? Can He bear its weight? Or is He liable to give up on us at some stage or otherwise fail to do what is necessary for our salvation? The Colossians had faith in the Christ, and so should we as we go through the trials of life. When our conscience strikes us, we should turn to Jesus. When we fail, become confused, frightened, or just plain despondent, we should turn to Him. He is human—one of us. He is divine—able to save.

The second reason why Paul gave God thanks as he prayed was that the Colossians had a love "for all the consecrated ones." The important word here is the word *all*, often misunderstood, as if Paul simply said he had heard merely of their love for fellow believers. *All* here, as in most cases in Scripture, means "without distinction." The Colossians' love was inclusive. It included Jews and Gentiles, men and women, people from any social status. It was a love that did not distinguish, it realized and therefore demonstrated that, in Christ, there is no difference (Romans 3:22; 10:12; Galatians 2:6). Distinctions that were so much part of the fabric of Roman society and of Israel's thinking had no relevance in the church.

Yes, culture has its valid place, but where culture runs contrary to the gospel it is to be contradicted. Rome could not exist apart from the social structure it created and that sustained daily life. But from Paul's point of view, Rome had no right to exist if it was so thoroughly committed to ungodly concepts that it was incapable of changing. Rodney Starks's fascinating little book on the early church, *The Rise of Christianity*, demonstrates how the early Christians' inclusive, practical love amazed and challenged the Roman world.[4] The oft-quoted text, "By this all people will know that you are my disciples, if you have love for one another" (John 13:36), says as much.

This was a major issue in Paul's mind because Christian inclusiveness constituted a denial of all distinctions and thereby implied the grace of the gospel. Grace implied the sufficiency of Christ's achievement over and above human merit or failure. It further implied the primacy of Christ in the Christian life, including the life of the church.

The Colossians were not to be satisfied merely with believing the truth; they were to practice it. Grace was to be the foundation of all they

---

[4] Philippi was in Greece. Colossae was across the sea and to the south, in Asia Minor.

did, and grace expresses itself in sacrificial love. Sincere love can never be satisfied with warm emotions; it demands practical expression in the way we treat others. As John put it, "If anyone has the world's goods and sees his brother in need, yet closes his heart against him, how does God's love abide in him" (1 John 3:17)?

As we shall see, these themes occupy a central place in Paul's letter to the Colossians. The false teachers in Colossae denied Jesus' primacy by denying the sufficiency of His achievements and thereby inevitably questioned the unity of the church. They taught that conversion was to be followed by a higher level of enlightenment through abstinence, ritual, and the worship of angels. In this way they divided Christians into two camps: the enlightened, and all the rest. Paul refused to accept such a division because he knew Christ's work to be all-sufficient.

The Colossians' faith and love had a foundation, a solid source. They existed "because of the hope stored for you in the heavens." Paul elaborated on this idea in his letter to the Ephesians:

> He chose us in him before the creation of the world to be holy and blameless in his sight. In love he predestined us for adoption to sonship through Jesus the Christ, in accordance with his pleasure and will to the praise of his glorious grace, which he has freely given us in the one he loves. In him we have redemption through his blood, the forgiveness of sins in accordance with the riches of God's grace that he lavished on us. With all wisdom and understanding he made known to us to us the mystery of his will according to his good pleasure, which he purposed in Christ according to his good pleasure which he purposed in Christ, to be put into effect when the times reach their fulfillment—to bring unity to all things in heaven and on earth under Christ (1:4–10).

We are studying Colossians, so we will focus on what Paul had to say here, but there is little doubt that what Paul said in his letter to the Ephesians makes his intention here clearer. The Colossians' faith and love, particularly their love, had to do with their hope for the future, with what we now call eschatology. They loved all without distinction "because of the hope stored for them in the heavens" (Colossians 1:5), and that hope was for the accomplishment of God's purposes, "to be put into effect when the times reach their fulfillment," "to bring unity to all things in heaven and on earth under Christ" (Ephesians 1:10).

The false teachers insisted everything could be had in the here and now of life; there was no need to wait for what was to come. Paul insisted there is nothing more than Jesus. His achievements cannot be superseded. Paul further insisted that "we are saved by hope" (Romans 8:24). What we have now are but the firstfruits of the future, a future that lies in the hand of God and will not be forced until He decides its time has come.

Christians are always torn between present realities and their longing for perfection. The false teachers appealed to this valid longing. We humans tend to be impatient. The false teachers manipulated this weakness. They promised everything at once. But God has a purpose for the history of the world, and He will not be hurried. That purpose is the mystery that makes sense of it all, and we should rest in the confidence of God's sure hand as He guides our history and that of the world.

Paul elaborated on the mystery later on in Colossians when he claimed to suffer "for the sake of His body, which is the church" (1:24), in which the eternally intended unity of mankind is achieved, and

> of which I have become a servant in accordance with the responsibility God has given me for you, to accomplish the Word of God, the mystery that had been hidden from the beginning of the ages and from generations past, but has now been shown to His consecrated ones, to whom God wanted to make known what are the riches of the glory of this mystery among the nations [compare Ephesians 1:8–11; 2:11–3:6]. That mystery is Christ among you, Jews and Gentiles, the hope for the glory, whom we proclaim, warning every person and teaching every person with a full measure of wisdom, so we can present every person mature in Christ through the activity of Him who is powerfully active in me (1:25–29).

Paul's repeated emphasis on "every person" (1:28, 2:1) parallels the Colossians "love for all the consecrated ones, (1:4)" but we will come to that.

The false teachers in Colossae insisted on the existence of a mystery of spirituality, accessible only to the few and faithful. The mystery of which Paul spoke is not of that kind. Christian mystery is not a secret to which only the initiated have access; it is something not quite clear in the past but now clarified to all.

Paul had a large view of the church. He viewed the church as a harbinger of the future as God designed it to be, the "here and now" and the "already" of the "there and then," the "not yet" but is sure to be. The future has invaded the present, first in the person and work of Christ ("If it is by the Spirit of God that I cast out demons, then the kingdom of God has come upon you" [Matthew 12:28]), and second in the life and witness of the church. History has been knocked off its sinful course and forced back into the course of God's original design: all in Christ, all subject to God in Christ.

Of course, even that is not quite correct, but I'm sure my point is clear. Every detail of the history of the world is under the guiding hand of God. We've already made reference to God's eternal purpose. Now we're discussing the practical implications of that purpose. Since God eternally intended to bring all under Christ, Satan's apparent victories can only serve that purpose. Even what appears to be a deviation from God's eternal purposes serves to that end: God intended the world to be united in Christ through the gospel, on the grounds of grace, and He will achieve exactly that. Grace is the means by which God has chosen to glorify Himself. Grace is the ground of our salvation, the grounds on which the church was formed, and the grounds on which we are to conduct church life "to the praise of his glorious grace" (Ephesians 1:6).

That is what makes church life so important, and that is what makes how we do church so important. Truly biblical church life focuses on God and His glory. That is the purpose for which the world was created. We must be characterized, like the Colossians, by a "love for all the consecrated ones." Race, culture, color, social standing, language, doctrinal preference—these and many other distinctions must not be allowed to divide us. No one and nothing but Him should characterize us. All who are consecrated by God for Himself are our brothers and sisters. We must actively love them by coming alongside them, living with them, serving, and worshipping God together without distinctions.

Is our love as bold and as inclusive? Do we really put God in Christ first as we formulate our choices, particularly with regard to church life? Do we seek to love or be loved, to honor God or be cuddled? Do we seek to give, to forbear, to forgive, and to encourage, or are we busy measuring churches by how much they give us? Does our church draw us closer to God or to ourselves? Is the preaching in our churches focused on glorifying God or meeting human expectations? These are fundamental questions we must ask ourselves in this selfish, me-first generation that has lost so much of the power of the gospel because it has lost so much of God in its strivings and aspirations.

The hope that informed the Colossians' love was, Paul said, "stored" by God "for you in the heavens." Note: the hope stored for the Colossians was "in the heavens." It was not an earthly hope. It did not have to do with future earthly circumstances but with those in heaven.

It was stored, kept secure "where neither moth nor rust destroys and where thieves do not break in and steal" (Matthew 6:20), by the reliability of the One who did the storing. Paul was saying that whatever God purposes, He will achieve, and whatever blessings He intends for His people, they will enjoy. God in Christ is the faithful guardian of those blessings. Still further, the apostle assured the Colossian Christians that God had them in mind when He stored those blessings. The church is not an afterthought, nor was the salvation of any one of the Colossians incidental. God not merely stored His blessings, but he did so with certain people in mind.

We must hear the same message today: the hope that stirs our hearts and shapes our church life is stored in the heavens *for us*. If God's purposes were directed at everyone in general, they could not have been for anyone in particular. Paul believed God has individuals in mind and specific communities (such as the Colossians). He had, therefore, not merely stored the hope, but stored it for them (I hope you, dear reader, are included, which you are if you are in Christ) because it was eternally meant for them. They were to encourage themselves with the thought. When faced with the difficulties sin created, they were to remind themselves God had them and their circumstances in mind. Regardless of the difficulties, victory was stored for them, secure in heaven.

You can see, then, how a truly biblical eschatology informs practice, provides direction, and creates spiritual and moral muscle. The doctrine of the last things is not meant to satisfy curiosity or titillate feelings. It is meant to shape things in the present. Is that how you treat prophecy? Is that what eschatology does for you, or are you more interested in getting a handle on things? What impact does your eschatology have on your daily life?

Paul went on to say that the Colossians were informed of that hope when Epaphras first preached the gospel to them. Eschatology is part of the gospel because the gospel has to do with sin, which is disobedience, and with God-centered obedience, which is holiness and an affection for God. Creation and eschatology are related through the gospel because eschatology is salvation worked out in full, and salvation is nothing less than the restoration of all things to their original purpose. That is also what eschatology is about: the subjection of all and everything to the glory of God. So, with reference to the hope, Paul said to the Colossians that it is a hope "of which you heard earlier through the truthful word of the gospel."

One important result of sin is the animosity that exists between people. We are adept at justifying our arrogance and the rejection of any who are unlike us. Ever since Adam tried to lay the blame of his sin on Eve, we human beings have been at loggerheads one with another. Adam betrayed his wife. Cain murdered his brother. Lemech celebrated his cruel, selfish pride in a song (Genesis 4:23–24), and a short while later the earth was filled with violence (Genesis 6:11, 13), and so the story continues.

The history of the world is the history of man contending with man, nation suppressing nation. Warfare has been the most pronounced impetuses in human progress, leading to research and development more than any other factor. The kingdom of Satan is divided against itself. Mankind is at war with itself, but the gospel establishes peace with God and peace among men by putting God's glory first and, in this way, providing mankind with a common aspiration, the grounds for living together in love and generous kindness.

Imagine a world in which all nations are devoted to the glory of God. Imagine a world in which discussions at the United Nations are not the product of selfish national interests but of a shared desire to honor God by doing good one to another. The gospel begins with God and His purposes and concludes with the achievement of those purposes, calling the consecrated to live in their light and assuring them of those purposes' accomplishment.

This is not merely a gospel, good news. It is "the truthful word of the gospel," in tune with God, in tune with reality by challenging and transforming it, in tune with reality as it will assuredly be in the Ultimate Future. The gospel of Christ can and should be trusted. We can and should stake our lives on it, live by it, and rest in its promises.

It is also the true gospel in contrast with the Colossian heresy, which, instead of uniting, divided; instead of focusing on God, called Christians to focus on themselves; instead of pointing to the sufficiency of Christ, invited the Colossians to improve on Christ's work by adding their own efforts. The result would inevitably be pride, self-satisfaction, deceit, and contention.

The gospel, Paul said, "is coming to you as it also does in all the world." It "is coming"— present tense—because it was still spreading in Paul's day, as it is in ours. Epaphras' gospel, also taught by Paul, was the gospel that was being spread "in all the world." The apostle was affirming that what he had to say to them was compatible with what they had heard originally from Epaphras; that what they heard from Epaphras was exactly what he taught, and that the two taught no foreign gospel but were teaching the truth of God. There was no disparity between Paul, Epaphras, and any true teacher of the gospel.

There was, however, substantial disparity between what Paul and Epaphras were teaching and the teachings of the Colossians' new teachers.

New ideas are more likely mistaken than true. Can it be that no one, anytime, anywhere discovered what you, or the Colossian teachers discovered? Do you really think it is likely that all the Christians in all the world, in all generations, were unable to see what Mr. Wonderful has discovered? The gospel is too wide, too deep, and too comprehensive to be perfectly understood by any one individual, church, or generation. As Bernard of Chartres put it, "We are dwarfs perched on the shoulders of giants. Thus we see more things than they did and farther than they did, not because our sight is sharper or our height greater, but because they lift us into the sky and raise us up by means of their gigantic stature."

In order to grow, we need a healthy dose of humility. We need to follow Paul's example and advice when he said, "If anyone thinks he knows something, he does not yet know as he ought to know" (1 Corinthians 8:2). In that spirit he wrote later to the church in Philippi,

> Not that I have already obtained this or am already perfect, but I press on to make it my own because Christ Jesus has made me his own. Brothers, I do not consider that I have made it my own. But one things I do: forgetting what lies behind and straining forward to what lies ahead, I press on toward the goal for the prize of the upward calling of God in Christ Jesus. Let those of us who are mature think this way, and if in anything you think otherwise, God will reveal that also to you. Only let us hold true to what we have attained (Philippians 3:12–15).

One way we can live with others as we ought, has to do with the recognition that we have a good deal to learn and that we can be made wiser by all our teachers (Psalms 119:99).

That is part of the value of church life, of living in the fellowship of those with whom we disagree. Such disagreements challenge. They drive us to study further, to think more carefully, and to pray a good deal more. They are opportunities for growth in which we come to realize that the truth is wider than our minds, that there are aspects of truth others are better equipped to see.

With that in mind, Paul described the gospel as "coming" to the Colossians "as it also does in all the world." The Colossians were not the only recipients of grace. The world was being impacted by the gospel. Of course, "all the world" is hyperbole. Paul did not mean to be understood literally. He was making a point. He was indicating the broad expanse of the gospel's impact. Note, too, how Paul spoke of the gospel: it is not being brought but is "coming." It has a life of its own, a power to change the world.

Paul was inviting the Colossians to compare the false doctrines of the purported teachers with what other Christians "in all the world" believed. If you think you've discovered something no one else has ever seen, you will have an inflated sense of importance and, again, you are more likely to be wrong than right.

The gospel that came to the Colossians and to many others was "bearing fruit and growing." Individuals and communities were being transformed. Slaves' suppressed dignity was reasserted. Slave owners' arrogance was being challenged and replaced with kindness, respect, and the fear of God (read the letter to Philemon and you'll get a sense of what I'm talking about). Jews and Gentiles related to one another as equals between whom there was no difference (read the book of Galatians and see how that came about). Women were accorded the social and religious same privileges as men. Unwanted babies were no longer thrown away like refuse. The weak were nurtured, the sick were tended, and the poor were fed. Men and women who formerly had no interest in God were moved to love Him, and those devoted to ritual were taught the importance of sincere devotion.

"As it also does among you from the day you heard and fully and truly experienced the grace of God." The Colossians were likewise impacted from the get-go, from the very first day they heard and "heard and fully and truly experienced the grace of God." It is not enough to know about grace. The grace of God needs to be *experienced*. Gospel grace is not so much a doctrine as it is a personal relationship with God and with one another. It is possible to be a superb theologian, to dot all the doctrinal i's and cross all the theological t's, yet know nothing of the reality of God's grace.

Do *you* know grace? Is your knowledge merely theoretical, or have you "heard and fully and truly experienced the grace of God"? Believe me, dear reader; that is one of the most important questions I can ask. Your eternal destiny hangs on an honest answer. So search your heart and answer in the presence of God.

Grace is kindness in the absence of merit. It is the very contrast of what the Colossian false teachers sought to promote. They spoke of going beyond grace, beyond Christ, beyond forgiveness and redemption to spiritual achievement. Paul (and Epaphras) spoke of grace, affirming there was nothing beyond what grace provided. No human achievement can accomplish what grace has accomplished for and in us.

"As you learned from Epaphras." Once again we are reminded that Paul's letter is firmly established in historical reality. The Colossians were not residents of an imaginary never-never land that existed once upon a time. They actually existed and actually heard the gospel from an actual person whose name was Epaphras, the abbreviated form of Epaphroditus—a common name at the time. The New Testament knows of another individual by the same name (Philippians 2:25; 4:18), a member of the church in Philippi,[5] but of the Colossian Epaphras we know nothing beyond what Paul said here and in verse 23 of Philemon. The Colossians knew, and that is all that counts.

Epaphras was "beloved" of Paul. *Beloved* is a term the apostle used quite often—twenty-nine times, twenty-six of which referred to fellow believers. Four times in his letters, he encouraged Christians to greet one another with a kiss (Romans 16:12; 1 Corinthians 16:20; 2 Corinthians 13:12; 1 Thessalonians 5:26). He insisted on telling the Corinthians that he loved them (2 Corinthians 11:11; 12:15), and the end of his letter to the Romans is full of expressions of appreciation and affection to twenty-eight individuals, not taking into account groups of individuals he mentioned as well. Paul was far from the coldhearted individual some imagine him to be. If we take into further account the 116 times he addressed his fellow believers as brothers, we gain further insight into this remarkable man's life. He was a man in love with God. He was also a person who enjoyed close personal relations with others whom he held in high regard.

---

[5] Rodney Stark, *The Rise of Christianity: How the Obscure, Marginal Jesus Movement Became the Dominant Religious Force in the Western World in a Few Centuries* (San Francisco: Harper, 1997).

He was truly a warmhearted man. Loving God, he loved his fellow man. His affection for those with and among whom he labored was superseded only by his affection for God. His devotion to the community of believers, the church, is amazing, as we shall see further in what follows. Do we dare be as affectionate and as committed? Do we express our affection, or have we been persuaded by the false view that affection is effeminate, or somehow sub-Christian?

As we noted with reference to Timothy, Paul treated those with whom he served as equals. Epaphras is described as "our beloved fellow-slave who is a faithful servant of Christ for your sake." Paul could have chosen to describe him as his assistant, or his understudy. He could have used some other term to distinguish himself from Epaphras ("young Epaphras," for example). But Paul was not interested in promoting himself. He was interested in the glory of Christ and in promoting others in the service of Christ. So Epaphras is not only "beloved" and not only a "fellow-slave," but he also commended as "a faithful servant of Christ for your sake." This commendation gives us a sense of what we should all be like. We should serve God in Christ by promotion, not for self-satisfaction, but for their sake.

"Who also described to us your sincere (or, hearty) love." What Paul knew of the church, he learned from others. As we saw, he was not the church's founder, nor had he visited the church by the time he wrote this letter.

LET'S SUMMARIZE

- Jesus is the Father's beloved, and should be ours. He is fully God, Lord of creation and salvation.

- Our focus should be on Christ in whom all is to be found. He is to be preeminent in everything we do, because the Father has made Him preeminent in all that He does in the world.

- God's grace is the grounds of everything Christian. Christian unity between those who differ is a vivid demonstration of grace. Christian love must embrace all who are in Christ—in practice, not merely in theory.

- Eschatology properly understood motivates to morality; the church is to exemplify what the future holds in Christ.

LET'S PRAY

Eternal God,

whose purposes determine all things

and who has purposed to undo the consequences of sin,

we revel in expectation of the hope

secured for us by Christ in heaven

and seek Your help to live on earth

in accordance with that hope.

Help us love Your Son above all

and accord Him the preeminence in our lives,

both private and congregational.

Teach us to love all those whom You love

and welcome them as You welcomed us,

for the glory of Christ through the gospel, amen.

QUESTIONS FOR DISCUSSION AND STUDY:

1. Discuss the mixture of humility and authority Paul exercised. What practical lessons are we to learn from his example?

2. What are the practical implications of the preeminence and lordship of Christ in church life?

3. Scan and summarize what Paul has to say about eschatology in this letter and indicate how your findings should impact your church's conduct.

4. What is the realtion between eschatology and the doctrine of salvation in this letter?

5. From what we have learned in this section, what is the value and importance of church life?

CHAPTER 2

The Wonder of Salvation Is the Wonder of the Savior
(COLOSSIANS 1:9–23)

9 Because of that we too, from the day we heard of it, do not stop praying for you and asking that you might be filled with a thorough knowledge of His will with every kind of spiritual wisdom and understanding, 10 so as to behave in a way that is worthy of the Lord, fully pleasing Him in every good deed, bearing fruit and growing in the thorough knowledge of God, 11 strengthened with every kind of strength in proportion to the power of His glory to endless endurance and fortitude with joy, 12 giving thanks to the Father, who made you fit for a portion in the inheritance of the consecrated ones in light, 13 who rescued us from the authority of the darkness and transferred us into the kingdom of the Son of His love 14 in whom we have the redemption, the forgiveness of sins, 15 who is the visible expression of the invisible God, firstborn in relation to all creation 16 because by Him was created everything that exists in the heavens and on the earth, visible and invisible, kings or powers or rulers or authorities.

Everything was created through Him and for Him, 17 and He is prior to everything, and everything holds together by Him, 18 and He is the head of the body—of the church—who is the firstborn from the dead so that in everything He might have the prior place

19 because in Him the fullness of deity was pleased to reside, 20 and through Him to reconcile everything to Himself, establishing peace through the blood of His cross—through Him, be it things on the earth or the things in the heavens.

21 And you, then, were alienated and enemies in the mind by your wicked deeds, 22 but He has reconciled you through His fleshly body and through His death so as to present you before Him holy, unblameable and free from rebuke 23 if in fact you continue steadfast in the Faith after having been firmly established, not subject to being moved away from the hope of the gospel of which you heard, and which is declared in all creation under heaven, of which declaration I, Paul, became a servant.

"Because of that," because of the Colossians' hearty faith and inclusive love of which Paul learned, "we too," in addition to unknown others, "from the day we heard of it, do not stop praying for you." We sometimes neglect to pray unless we need something. Paul was in Rome, under house arrest, awaiting Imperial decision as to whether he should live or die. But his prayers did not focus on his needs; he prayed for the Colossians.

There was not much he could do for the Colossians but write and pray, and he did both. He knew he could reach beyond the boundaries of his detention and touch the lives of the Colossians in prayer, so he prayed. He knew he could help them by writing, so he wrote. We should be immensely grateful that Paul did not allow his circumstances to cloud his vision. But, then, how could he? He knew Christ. He knew the gospel, and he had received encouraging news about the church in Colossae. He was so thrilled with what he heard that he was driven to prayer.

Do we forget to pray? Why do we pray? What do we pray for? Are we the kind of people or the kind of church that move people to pray for us in a positive way Paul prayed for the church in Colossae – does the quality of our church life move others to thank God?

Note what the apostle sought for the Colossians. Here we come to one of those lengthy, never-ending sentences, an expression of Paul's fertile mind, his lively heart, and the eagerness of his desires for the Colossian believers: "Asking that you might be filled with a thorough knowledge of his will with every kind of spiritual wisdom and understanding."

In this letter (and elsewhere), Paul used the terms all and filled as superlatives. I've tried to understand the point of each use and have translated it variously as "every kind," "endless," and such like. Please keep in mind that these are all efforts to convey a sense of the apostle's consistent use of the Greek term for "all" (or "full").

What did Paul request for the Colossians? "That you might be filled with a thorough knowledge of His will with every kind of spiritual wisdom and understanding." Before we look into the content of Paul's prayer, we would do well to ask why he makes such a request. After all, are spiritual advancement and understanding not the products of an individual's devotion, sacrifice, obedience, and persistence?

Well, yes and no. Above all, such advancement is the product of God's blessing on human effort. In and of itself, human effort can neither secure blessing nor achieve anything apart from it. Knowledge, spiritual wisdom, and understanding are not obtained by human effort, not even strenuous prayer. They are gifts from God and result in a life worthy of the gospel, which in turn leads to still greater knowledge. We have no right to expect to grow in our spiritual lives unless we exert ourselves to that end, but we would be foolish to think that anything of value in our spiritual lives can be obtained merely by our efforts. As with the advancement of the gospel and the health of a church, one man sows, another waters, but it is God who gives the increase. We cannot force God's hand to satisfy our desires.

That is the logic of Paul's request that they "be filled." Spiritual filling is something God does for us, not something we do for ourselves. We do not have the resources from which to draw, but His resources are plenteous. That is why Paul prayed for the Colossians as he did, just as he thanked God for their faith and love. He sought God on their behalf.

Paul asked that they be "filled with a thorough knowledge of His will with every kind of spiritual wisdom and understanding." In speaking of God's will, Paul did not have in mind an individual plan for each of us: whom we should marry, where we should live, what kind of schooling or employment we should take up, or where we should place our investments. Paul was referring to the ultimate will of God mentioned earlier, the mystery of God's will to unite everything under Christ.

The apostle would have the Colossians equipped with a "thorough knowledge" of God's will. But he was not satisfied with their mere possession of data. He wanted them to have this knowledge "with every kind of spiritual wisdom and understanding." That is to say, he wanted them to understand God's intentions and to relate to those intentions in a wise, spiritual manner. He wanted them to desire what God desires, love what God loves, and lead the kind of lives that are driven by those desires.

That, in fact, is Paul's next point. Information is important. We need to know in order to understand, and we need to understand in order to conduct ourselves properly. The Christian Faith is not empty intellectualism any more than it is merely emotionalism, however sincere. Nor is it groundless exhortation or imposed behavior. Christianity encourages thought. It creates intellectual curiosity and leads to intellectual development. The Colossians were not expected to be dependent on a priest or a rabbi to tell them what to do; they were to be "filled with every kind of spiritual wisdom and understanding" for a specific and very practical purpose: "so as to behave in a way that is worthy of the Lord, fully pleasing him in every good deed." Lightfoot put it succinctly: "The end of all knowledge, the Apostle would say, is conduct."[6] Their lives should have been in tune with what they knew. To such an end they needed "spiritual wisdom and understanding."

Think of it for a moment: Paul actually believed human beings can "behave in a way that is worthy of the Lord" and even please Him by their good deeds. If that is not grace, I don't know what is! Paul further believed such behavior was a human duty, the natural aspiration of the Colossian Christians. Is it yours? Are you grateful for the stupendously high calling to "behave in a manner that is worthy of the Lord"? That is a life worth living. There is more to life than eating, drinking, enjoying, or suffering. We should choose to live for something—for someone—far greater than ourselves, for the glory of God, "fully pleasing Him in every good deed."

Here comes grace again. Who can fully please the Lord? Whose conduct is so perfect that God cannot but be pleased with Him? No one, of course, but Jesus. Only He could say that He always does those things that please the Father (John 8:29). But such is the goal we must set ourselves, and when we fail (for fail we will, endless times), we must rely on God's grace and kindness to accept our feeble efforts and to render them acceptable by the virtues of Christ. When we hear, "Well done, good and faithful servant, enter into the joy and your Lord" (Matthew 25:21), we will know full well that we are, in truth, "unprofitable servants" (Luke 17:10) and that it is grace that accepts our feeble efforts with such kindness.

---

[6] Lightfoot, *Saint Paul's Epistles to the Colossians and Philemon*, 139.

When we aspire to live like that and rest on such assurances, we will discover that, like the Colossians, we will be "bearing fruit and growing in the thorough knowledge of God." The fruit we will bear is the holiness of our lives and the acts of kindness that issue from our understanding of the gospel. As we behave in such a manner, we shall also grow "in the thorough knowledge of God." Life experiences, walking with God, and serving Him in the conduct of our lives will provide us with an ever-increasing personal acquaintance with Him. As a result, we will be further "strengthened with every kind of strength."

God never leaves us to cope on our own. He watches over us, lifts us when we fall, and strengthens us when we fail. He provides us with "every kind of strength" needed for every kind of task he has laid on us. He never requires of us what He will not enable us to do. Do you need fortitude to cope with difficulties as you serve Him? He will provide it. Do you need a thicker skin to bear the aspersions and unkind actions of others as you serve Him? He will provide. Do you need to be able to concentrate as you prepare a Sunday school lesson while the children are raising a ruckus? He will provide. Do you need more self-restraint as you seek to respond to provocations in a Christ-like manner? God will provide. He will strengthen you with "every kind of strength." But note: He does not promise to do so for other purposes. This is not a blank check, to be cashed at will. It is meant for those who seek to "behave in a way that is worthy of the Lord" and will fully please Him.

For such a tremendous goal we need more than "every kind of strength"; we need a good deal of it. That too is assured. God is generous toward us beyond expectation. Paul told the Colossians that when they exert themselves to such an end, God will provide them with strength "in proportion to the power of His glory."

That is quite a proportion! Think of the biblical descriptions of God's appearances. At Sinai, the mountain shook, thunder rolled, lightning flashed, a thick cloud appeared on the mountain, and a very loud trumpet blast sounded, so that all the people in the camp trembled (Exodus 19:16). Recall Nahum's description of the coming of the Lord:

> His way is in whirlwind and storm, and the clouds are the dust of his feet. He rebukes the sea and makes it dry; he dries up all the rivers; Bashan and Carmel wither; the bloom of Lebanon withers. The mountains quake before him; the hills melt; the earth heaves before him, the world and all who dwell in it. Who can stand be-

fore his indignation? Who can endure the heat of his anger? His wrath is poured out like fire, and the rocks are broken into pieces by him (Nahum 1:3–6, ESV).

Read Ezekiel Chapter One. There you will find a description of the "proportion" of "the power of His glory," and that is the proportion of the strength He provides to enable us to live to His glory.

Notice Paul said that the power God provides has a goal: "to endless endurance and fortitude with joy." It is not for the ability to work miracles, change reality for our comfort, free us from hardships, or transform life into an eternal garden of joys. That is yet to be. At the moment, we are to live in this world as it is, and to behave in a manner worthy of God in spite of the moral and spiritual environment, in spite of mocking glances and unkind responses. We are strengthened to endure these with a combination of "fortitude" and "joy."

Endure. Not escape, but endure with the kind of positive attitude to life, with the confident hope that the gospel provides, so that our endurance is characterized by joy rather than self-pity, bitterness, or any other unworthy response. We are not to be as occupied with our pains, sorrows, or hopes as much as we are to be occupied with Christ. We should have what Moule described as "a heart at leisure from itself." For that reason, we are to be free from the desire to seek revenge. We can turn the other cheek, go the extra mile, and bear with kindness the insults thrown against us, as our Lord did for our sake. We take our example from Him, who suffered endlessly for the joy that was set before Him.

We suffer with joy because we do not focus on our fears, pains, and losses but on Christ, His will, and His glory. We are not bound to the things of this world but to Jesus, not to security on earth but to the confidence we have in the inheritance purchased for us by the blood of the Christ. That is how the world is overcome. That is how the gospel is preached through our lives. That is how we demonstrate the reality of a faith that believes the present state of this world is about to change, that this world's values are mistaken, and that God and our fellow humans are worthy of being loved and sacrificially served.

Paul went on to spell out the source of this joy: "Giving thanks to the Father, who made you fit for a portion in the inheritance of the consecrated ones in light." The source of their joy was an understanding of the gospel. The Colossians knew they were unworthy of God's goodness. They were not naturally fit, nor did they achieve a standard that rendered them fit. They were made fit. God did for them what they could not do for themselves, which is also why they could consider the inheritance secure. It was not gained by their suitability; nor could it be lost by their unsuitability. Their inheritance was obtained by grace, safely stored in heaven for them.

In other words, the Colossians' understanding of the truth (*truth* is but another word for the gospel) was the source of their joy. They understood, even if it was not yet a conscious understanding, that such an inheritance was not to be obtained through mystical experiences, abstinence, indulgence, or ceremonial acts, even if somehow related to ancient Jewish custom. Nor did they consider such a privilege to be limited to a select few. They understood grace made it the domain of all who are in Christ. The Colossians' inheritance had been purchased by Christ and now awaited them.

In 3:4, Paul spelled out that inheritance. Here we'll just say the Father has changed our hearts and inclined them toward Himself. He sent His Holy Spirit to dwell within us, alter our priorities, teach us to delight in His law, and give us a hope that overcomes the world. The "inheritance of the consecrated ones," an inheritance that is enjoyed in the "light" of His glorious presence, has been secured for us.

That is the value of theology. That is the point of study and thought about the truths of the gospel. That is how we sink deep roots into the soil of the Word of God and secure ourselves from a sincere but questionable emotionalism that exposes us to non-biblical influences or a rationalism ignorant of spiritual realities.

Light was another term used by the false teachers. Those who accepted their teachings and followed them were said to have entered the light. They knew what others could not. They were the enlightened ones. But Paul credited the light to Jesus and His accomplishments on behalf of Christians, not to human merit.

Of this inheritance, said Paul, we receive a portion, a part. None have it all on their own. Its fullness can only be enjoyed in fellowship with others, with *all* the consecrated ones.

Next, Paul described how God made the Colossians fit for such an inheritance: The Father "rescued us from the authority of the darkness and transferred us into the kingdom of the Son of His love." We were under "the authority of the darkness" until the Father "rescued us." Note that Paul moved from *you* to *us.* He too partook of these saving blessings.

"The authority of darkness" is the realm where sin and Satan rule, to which realm mankind has been delivered because of the sin of Adam.

Darkness is the opposite of the light in which the consecrated ones receive "the inheritance." As servants of darkness, we could only do what darkness commanded, enjoying only those liberties the darkness allowed. Nor could we save ourselves. But the Father could and did, "and transferred us into the kingdom of the Son of his love."

In Romans, Paul described the same situation under different terms. Due to the sin of Adam, we were made subject to sin. We became its servants, obliged to do its bidding. Due to the righteousness of Christ—His perfect life on our behalf, His atoning death and resurrection—we are free from the guilt of Adam's sin and therefore from its consequences. In his letter to the Romans, Paul said that, in Christ, "we have the redemption." We are free from the law of sinning and dying. Christ has made us free, and He has done that so we can serve God in newness of spirit by fulfilling the righteousness of the Law through our daily conduct. Sin has no authority over us. We are the children of God, subject to grace, and if children, then heirs and joint heirs with Christ. We have "redemption, the forgiveness of sins."

Redemption speaks of the freeing of those once enslaved. Slavery was a status in Rome. Slaves could redeem themselves from slavery and achieve the status of freemen, but no sinner can redeem himself from the bondage of sin. The redemption we have is from God. As a result, our chains are broken. Our hearts are free. We have redemption. We do not have to sin. We do not have to obey the lusts of our bodies. We can lead holy, godly, spiritually minded lives, tend to the cultivation of our walk with God, and grow in knowledge of Him. We are no longer under the authority of the darkness; we have been transferred. We have been brought "into the kingdom of the Son of His love."

In a very real sense, the kingdom of God has come, and those who are in Christ have been brought in to it. Jesus reigns over them to sanctify, protect, guide, and secure them. Jesus is also Lord of all events, as the book of Revelation so gloriously shows. Every event comes from His hand, even the frustrated fury of the enemy.

There is, of course, a sense in which the kingdom is a matter for the future. Its fullest realization is yet to be. But what will be is based on what already is in Christ. We noted earlier and remind ourselves here: the future is in fundamental continuity with the present because eschatology is nothing less than salvation fully realized, Christology in full bloom. That is our inheritance, and it is yet to be realized.

Redemption, the forgiveness of sins, is a gloriously full salvation, the product of the work of a capable savior, whom Paul is about to describe.

Before we see what he has to say of Christ our Savior, let us note that those who are forgiven are those who are redeemed. Forgiveness of sins, salvation, is equal to freedom from sin and submission to the lordship of Christ.

Paul had begun to describe Jesus in an earlier reference when he spoke of him as "the Son of His [that is, of the Father's] love." God the Father loves the Son; that is clear. But it is possible that the natural love of the Father to the Son is not the only aspect of what is in view here. The context has to do with the saving work of Christ. Paul seemed to be speaking of Jesus as the object of the Father's love in His capacity as the Christ, the one who became flesh and dwelt among us, lived as one of us yet was without sin, and died on the cross, bearing the sin of the world to bring us to God. For example, it is in this sense Matthew applies the title "Son of God" to Jesus when, in 3:17 and again in 17:5, he described God as saying of Christ, "This is my beloved son in whom I am well pleased." The Greek uses a different word in each case, but the idea is identical.

So too, in John's Gospel, Jesus spoke of Himself as the Son and as the beloved of the Father with reference to His doing the will of the Father (John 3:16, 35; 5:19–26; and many others) rather than in terms of their shared divine nature.

In this capacity Christ Jesus is also "the visible expression of the invisible God." After all, the visibility of which Paul spoke is the product of the incarnation. By taking on humanity, including a human body, Christ became the visible expression of the invisible God. The Greek word rendered here "visible expression" is the word from which we get our word *icon*, often (correctly) translated "image." An image or icon is a visible representation of a person or a concept. As the apostle John put it, "The word became flesh and dwelt among us, and we have seen His glory, glory as of the only son from the Father, full of grace and truth... No one has ever seen God; the only God, who is at the Father's side, He has made Him known" (John 1:14, 18). That is the logic of our Lord's claim: "He who has seen me, has seen the Father" (John 14:9). Jesus revealed God in order to save. Salvation has to do with a true knowledge of God (John 17:3).

The next phrase has been a bone of contention. It can be purportedly translated either as including Jesus within creation or as setting Him in contrast to creation: either as the firstborn of all created things or as the firstborn in relation to all created things. The following phrase seems to resolve the difficulty because it states that Christ created everything, and shortly thereafter that everything was created through Him. Surely, He was not His own creator. As in all of Jesus' actions, He is the agent of the Father, who created the "all" that exists by way of the Son. Absolutely everything created is said to have been created by Christ and for Him.

We conclude, then, that Paul was pointing to Jesus' unique position: Christ enjoys the status of firstborn in relation to creation as a firstborn does in relation to his siblings. But He is not one of His siblings; He stands on His own in relation to them. His is the double portion. He is the authority among His brothers. He holds primary position.

There was a reason for this insistence on Paul's part. The Colossians were being challenged by a religious theory of divine emanations that later developed into a cult. According to this theory, the material world is the lowest level of existence, inherently evil and created by a demigod (known as the demiurge), the lowest of a series of emanations known as "the fullness" (*pleroma* in Greek). This series was said to climax in the unseen, wholly spiritual god. Paul was saying that the incarnated Christ, the Jesus who walked on earth in a human body, ate and slept, taught and was crucified, is none other than the gloriously supreme being at the top of the divine ladder, and that there is not an iota of Godhood that does not belong to Him.

Of course, the apostle did not accept the theory of divine emanations. All he was saying was that whatever was attributed by the false teachers to the supreme God is to be attributed to Jesus. Did the Colossians aspire to know God? That is a commendable aspiration that should characterize every Christian. The way to know God is to focus on Jesus because He "is the visible expression of the invisible God." God is not to be sought elsewhere but in Christ. He cannot be known elsewhere, and all pretensions of knowledge beyond the knowledge He provides are false.

Paul presented a glorious view of Jesus' deity a very short while after Jesus was crucified, buried, and rose from the dead. It is a simple fact of history that faith in the deity of Christ preceded any doubt of His deity. What was questioned first was His humanity (1 John 4:1–3). Those who knew Him most intimately, like His brother James, did not hesitate to put Him on the same par as God the Father (James 1:1), address Him as Lord (James 1:1; 2:1), and ascribe to Him clearly divine designations such as "the Glory" (See in the Greek of James 2:1; compare Psalms 24:7–10). His divinity was so obvious that they took it for granted. Only His humanity was doubted.

It was Paul's desire to undermine every inkling of foundation for the false teaching promoted in Colossae. He realized the best way to do that was to present the truth in a positive way before attacking the error. So he presented the truth about Jesus, indirectly addressing the errors of the false teachers by enlisting their terminology and referring to their assumptions. Jesus is God made visible by way of a human body and the life conducted in that body. He is God made visible by His death and resurrection. Jesus is the one by whom we come to know God.

Paul went on to explain why Jesus is the firstborn in relation to creation: "Because by Him was created everything that exists in the heavens and on the earth." Obviously "everything" excludes Jesus. At the same time "everything" points to Jesus as Creator. It insists that the one described in the first chapter of Genesis as commanding the world into being is Jesus the Christ. Paul has made as clear and as convincing a declaration of Jesus' deity as could be imagined.

His creative act is inclusive, as inclusive as the Colossians' love should be. Nothing that exists, in the heavens or on the earth, exists apart from Jesus. Note the plural, "heavens." Paul may well have been referencing the series of purported emanations, each in its descending level of heavens. He is encouraging the Colossians to view Jesus as their all in all.

To emphasize the inclusivity of Christ's creative activity, Paul detailed the description of created things in the heavens and on earth: "visible and invisible (and therefore human or spiritual), kings (literally thrones) or powers (literally lordships) or rulers or authorities." All four could refer to human or purported spiritual realities. Whatever they may be, Jesus is over them all; indeed, He is the Creator of them all. No power, no authority, no noble, governor, procurator, or king ruled in the heavens or on earth apart from the will of Christ.

"Everything was created through Him." Paul now introduced a new concept: what Jesus created, the Father created through Him. This is much like what Jesus said when He spoke of certain actions as done both by the Father and by Himself (John 5:17–27; 10:30–38; 14:9–24; 16:15). Inherent in these words is the doctrine of the Trinity, or at least the doctrine of the Oneness in essence of the Father and the Son.

Paul went further. Not only is Jesus fully God, the Creator of all that exists, speaking of the past; everything was created "for Him", speaking of the present and the future. The Greek actually could be translated as "all things were created unto Him"; that is, everything has its goal in

Jesus. The universe exists for Jesus and finds its logic in Him. History, personal and national, unfolds for Jesus, with Him in view and Him as the goal. The vicissitudes of life all have Him as their ultimate goal and culminate in relation to Him. Human life finds meaning in Him. For that reason, everything is out of sync unless it is in sync with Him.

This puts history, science, art, and everyday life on a different plain than we might expect: they all have Ultimate Meaning because their Ultimate Meaning is Christ. Christians should engage in each to the glory of God, and those who engage in any of these apart from faith in Christ are rebelling against Him, regardless of their conscious intentions. Life in all its aspects takes on wonderful meaning as well as tremendous import.

No wonder, then, that Paul said next of Jesus that "He is prior to everything." The priority spoken of is not chronological in the sense that he existed before all things. After all, Jesus could not have brought anything into existence unless He had that kind of priority. "He is prior to everything" in the sense that nothing is as important as He is. Nothing carries as much worth as He does. He must come first in all things because the ultimate priority is His. The reason for all that exists and occurs is to be found in Him.

"And everything holds together by Him." Lightfoot said of this verse that Jesus' activity in creation is what makes the universe "a kosmos rather than a chaos."[7] As Lord of all, Christ unites heaven and earth, the material and the spiritual. He is not only the universe's Creator and goal; He is also its logic. He keeps the world from falling apart. He ensures everything will ultimately be resolved into its divinely intended goal. He guides the course of history, keeps the heavenly bodies in their course, secures the processes of nature, and causes the tide to ebb and flow. Not a petal falls nor an egg hatches but by His command. That is what Hebrews 1:3 means when it says Jesus upholds all things by His powerful Word.

From a description of Christ in relation to salvation and to the world, Paul then turned to describe Him in relation to the church. William Hendriksen, in his book A Commentary on Colossians and Philemon drew attention to a fascinating parallelism between Christ's role in salvation and in the church by comparing verse 15 with 18, verse 16 with 19 and verse 17 with 20.[8]

[7] Lightfoot, Saint Paul's Epistles to the Colossians and Philemon, 156.

[8] William Hendriksen, A Commentary on Colossians and Philemon (London: The Banner of Truth Trust, 1971), 66.

Jesus is also "the head of the body—the church." Paul had spoken in the past of the church by comparing it with a body (Romans 12:4; 1 Corinthians 12:12–27), but here and his letter to the Ephesians are the only places in which he spoke of the church as an actual body. The metaphor is apt. Jesus' headship indicates His seniority, His rule, and the intimate relationship between Him and the church. The church is as dependent on Jesus as a body is on its head, without which it has neither life nor direction nor sight, without which it cannot breathe or obtain nourishment. It that sense, the head is the source of life to a physical body as Jesus is to the church. Jesus is the head of the church and the source of its life.

This Jesus "is the firstborn from the dead." Once again, chronology is not the point, except in the sense that the beginning of anything can also be its source. The title "firstborn" in this case relates to Jesus' priority by the nature of His resurrection in comparison with all who have risen or will ever rise: it is He who raises them. "As the father raises the dead and gives them life, so also the Son gives life to whom He will" (John 5:21 [see v. 26]; 6:27, 33, 40, 54). The resurrected are creatures, with no source of life apart from what He grants them. Jesus is their Creator, the source of their life. Just as He formed them in the womb and gave them life, just as he is the head of the church, so, too, He raises the dead, as Paul said in Colossians, "so that in everything He might have the prior place."

For Jesus to be "the firstborn from the dead" he must have also partaken of death. Now here is an amazing truth: He who died is the Lord of life and death. No wonder Peter said death could not hold on to Him. He is the source and power of the resurrection. That is why Paul did not describe Jesus as He who *was* the firstborn from the dead (past tense), but He who is (present tense). He will be the firstborn from the dead for all eternity.

Paul envisaged no life apart from Jesus. Nor should we. Paul could not envisage the Christian life except as it focuses on Jesus. Rather than there being a higher Christian life, any focus that is not on Christ is of a lower level. It does not matter if we are focused on holiness or dedication, on church growth or on spiritual gifts, on correct doctrine or on evangelism. Church life in which Christ does not fill the whole of one's vision is sub-Christian.

Paul was at pains to persuade the Colossians of Jesus' all-sufficiency. He wanted them to understand that there was no need to look for anything beyond Christ. Indeed, there is nothing beyond Him. Having put their faith in Jesus, the Colossians' task was to accord Him His due priority in all things. They were to focus on Him, not on anything else. Is that not a lesson modern Christians need to hear?

One would think that Paul had exhausted his topic, but a description of the incomparable Christ, however inspired, will exhaust human words before they are able to give a full sense of His true glory. So the apostle continues.

Another reason why Jesus is to be accorded priority in church life is because "in Him the fullness of deity was pleased to reside." The proponents of error in Colossae believed deity was a descending ladder of emanations, which was called "the fullness." Not so, insists Paul. Everything divine must be attributed to Jesus. Not only are there no graduations of deity; Jesus encompasses the "fullness of deity." Any characteristic, attribute, quality, power, essence, or form of being that may legitimately be associated with deity is to be found in Him. He is very God of very God, to use the ancient declaration.[9] He is not a lesser God because He is the Son; being the Son, He is in all respects equal in His nature with the Father.[10] Surely, such a One deserves priority.

Paul provided yet another reason to ascribe Jesus the most honorable place in our private and communal walk with God. Not only was the fullness of deity pleased to dwell in Jesus, but that deity was also pleased "through Him to reconcile everything to Himself, establishing peace." Everything is presently hostile to God; but everything is to be changed and reconciled to God. The ultimate purpose of creation is to be achieved "through Him"; that is, through Jesus. Indeed, He Himself is the ultimate purpose of creation. The resurrection of Jesus is the beginning of a new creation, of the redemption of "all things."

Once again we have our attention drawn to an important aspect of the Christian Faith, one in which it differed clearly from that of the heretical teachers in Colossae, as well as from the views of some modern Christians. The gospel has a very positive view of creation. Not only did God call the world into existence and proclaim it very good, but He intends to be glorified in and through it. Everything in creation is ultimately to benefit from the redemptive sacrifice of Christ the Savior

---

[9] The Nicene Creed, 325 BC.

[10] This is not the place to enter into a discussion of the trinity. Paul says nothing here about the Spirit, and since we are studying Colossians, not systematic theology, I have chosen to resist the strong temptation to answer questions Paul does not address in this letter.

(Read Romans Chapter 8 and note what Paul has to say there about the redemption of creation). "Everything"—once again that inclusive word that is so important in the letter to the Colossians.

Paul spoke again of eschatology, and he cannot do so apart from salvation. The salvation of individuals is not the goal of the gospel; it is a means to an end. Individuals are saved in order to be reconciled to God and so utterly transformed that they meet God's requirements. He will then no longer have reason to be in enmity with them. Everything has been affected by sin. The earth was cursed because of Adam's disobedience. The transformation of everything is the goal of Jesus' sacrificial death. Everything is to be redeemed, brought to its intended goal in Christ. Everything has already been brought under Christ, redemptively and not merely in terms of His sovereignty.

How was this achieved? "Through the blood of His cross." Whose blood? Whose cross? Familiarity has inured us to the impact of this last statement, which is as stupendous as anything we have seen so far in this letter. The blood and the cross of which Paul spoke are those of the Son in whom the fullness of deity was pleased to dwell. This brings to mind Paul's amazing, disturbing phrase used when he addressed the elders of the church in Ephesus. He spoke of "the church of God, which He obtained with His own blood" (Acts 20:28). God crucified. God's blood, shed. Could there be a starker, less likely statement than that? In case his readers did not get it, Paul reiterated: the He of whom he spoke earlier in such glowing terms, to whom he attributed creation, the goal and logic of all that exists, was none other than the Jesus who was killed on a cross in Jerusalem.

His death was not the final victory of His enemies; it was their overthrow. It was the means by which God in Christ achieved His purpose, reconciling sinners to Himself, establishing peace, and granting them redemption, the forgiveness of sins. It is the means by which God secured peace with all things, "be it things on the earth or the things in the heavens."

We can now see ever more clearly how soteriology (the doctrine of salvation) is the product of Christology (the doctrine of Christ's nature, person, and work), and that Christology issues into eschatology (the doctrine of the last things). High views of Christ lead to high views of Christ's accomplishments and therefore to high views of the salvation He obtained. Low views of Christ inevitably lead to a weakening of the gospel.

Paul now turned to his readers in Colossae: "And you, then, were alienated and enemies in the mind by your wicked deeds." Paul described the state of the Colossians prior to their conversion in terms of estrangement and animosity that expressed themselves in how the Colossians viewed God. Their minds were bent against Him. Of course, they were not alone in this sorrowful reality because such is the state of all mankind. What is more, their "wicked deeds," expressive of their minds, led them to further animosity in an effort to silence their consciences and justify the way they conducted themselves.

What we do impacts us no less than it impacts others. The Nazi murderers were corrupted by the atrocities they perpetuated. Their consciences were rendered immune to human suffering. They persuaded themselves that what they did was valid, in the interests of the highest— Aryan—portion of the human race. Their minds justified the horror of their deeds to the extent that they dared adopt the slogan "*Gott mit uns*" (God is with us).

"But He has reconciled you through His fleshly body and through His death." The Colossians did nothing; God in Christ did it all. What greater gap could be imagined, what wider abyss traversed? A holy God, deserving of mankind's most sincere affection and heartfelt devotion, a God who both demands and deserves that man love Him with all his heart, soul, mind, and strength, was hated by those whom He created for His glory. Instead of casting them into the hell they deserve, He chose to save. He sent His Son to live among them, lead the life they should have led, die the death they worked so consistently to earn, and "reconciled them through His fleshly body and through His death so as to present them before Him holy, unblameable and free from rebuke" Amazing! Breathtakingly amazing!

Salvation has holiness as its goal, it includes sanctification. The redeemed are saved from the power of sin to lead a life of dedication to God, which is exactly what holiness means. In spite of their "wicked deeds," salvation renders the sinful "unblameable and free from rebuke" because their guilt was laid on Jesus. He exhausted the claims of God's law against them by bearing their punishment in His own body on the tree.

"If in fact you continue steadfast in the Faith." In these days of fads and fashions in which a constant hankering after something new has become a way of life, Paul's *if* was highly relevant. Every so often someone in the church stumbles over a new discovery: if only the church were more contemporary, or more seeker-friendly, more evangelistic, or more family orientated, more this or that or the other, it would become an amazing success. As a result, today's church is running after its tail, spinning endlessly and getting nowhere. It has lost sight of the gospel. It no longer believes that the message is, in and of itself, the power of God. Sometimes it gives the impression that God is altogether out of the equation, except to bless us with riches, pleasure, and happiness in response to our achievements. The church has become so much like the world that it has no message, and there is precious little reason for anyone to be attracted to it. But the church's duty is as clear as it is simple: "continue steadfast in the Faith." The rest is in the hands of God.

This is the other side to God's work in saving sinners: they are to "continue steadfast in the Faith." It is not a case of God doing His part and man doing his. The *if* here does not mean the work of God is in any way contingent on the faithfulness of man. If it did, the work of God would be undone. *If* raises no doubt as to the outcome; it simply points to the consequence of God's saving work just as, in Galatians 3:4, Paul used the same term to indicate a sure reality.

Could Christians ever suffer for Christ in vain? Of course not. Yet in Galatians 3:2–3, Paul asked, "Let me ask you only this: Did you receive the Spirit by law-keeping or by hearing with faith? Are you so foolish? Having begun by the Spirit, are you now being perfected by the flesh?" Obviously, the answer to each of these questions is a resounding "No!" "So too, when he asks, did you suffer so many things in vain—if indeed it was in vain?" The answer is clearly the same; *if* in no way indicates uncertainty. It serves to indicate the result of God's saving work, and at the same time the duty incumbent on those who have been the object of that work. They are to "continue steadfast in the Faith."

It is with regard to the message of that Faith that Paul said, "Of which I, Paul, became a servant." We too must become the servants of that Faith.

Note: Paul did not speak of faith but of "the Faith." There is an important difference. To continue in faith means to continue to believe. To continue in the Faith means to be true to the content of the Faith they had originally heard from Epaphras. As Paul said, the faith "of which you heard and which is declared in all creation under heaven, of which declaration I, Paul, became a servant."

The Colossians were invited to inquire anywhere they wished. Nowhere else were the doctrines of the false teachers being taught by anyone recognized by the apostles. Wherever the gospel was sounded, what the Colossians had heard from Epaphras and now read from Paul was in tune with what others taught and believed. The Colossians were to adhere to the same doctrines. "After having been firmly established" in them by an act of God and through Epaphras' faithful teaching, they were not to be "subject to being moved away" from them, with particular reference to the content of "the hope of the gospel."

That hope, as we have seen, has to do with gathering all things under Christ, and for that reason, it is the exact opposite of the elitism that the false teachers in Colossae promoted. No less important, the hope points to the primacy of Christ, whereas the Colossian teachers of error claimed to be able to supplement Him.

Note the hyperbole. He said that the gospel was "declared in all creation under heaven." Obviously that was not literally true.

Does your concept of the gospel meet up with Paul's? Do you think of Jesus as highly as Paul did? Are you amazed at the wonder of His deity? Are you thrilled by the act of incarnation? Are you ashamed of your sin? Does the thought that He bore its guilt and suffered its due punishment move you to gratitude and service? Do you strive after holiness and are you laboring to deepen your understanding of the Faith instead of running off with every new-fangled doctrine in search of an easy path to spirituality? Is your hope for the future biblical: does it focus on Christ and does it include a significant emphasis on holiness?

This is the moment when we need to remind ourselves of a simple truth of which we most likely lost sight as we studied: verses 9–23 are a prayer. True, Paul had included the Colossians in his act of worship (v. 21), but these verses describe the content of Paul's prayer for them.

Wow! What a prayer this is. I wonder how much worship there is in our prayers. Paul had not asked for the Colossians' health or wealth, for their physical comfort, or for a resolution of their problems. He had not asked God to provide them with employment or a spouse, or to change the heart of an adversary. He had not even asked for their protection. What he sought from God on their behalf was spiritual enlightenment and a consequent spiritual walk. Paul was more concerned for their godliness than he was for their gold, for their spiritual progress rather than their career. To the extent we think Paul's priorities were right, are we convicted.

As he prayed, he could not but find himself drawn to worship because drawing near to God and engaging his mind with the glories of Christ, he could not help but adore Christ as he was reminded of the wonders he described. I confess, that is what happened to me as I studied and wrote about these verses. Could it be otherwise, with such a magnificent description of Christ and of the gospel?

Let's Summarize

- Spiritual filling is a gift of God, not the fruit or reward of human effort, not even effort in prayer.

- Truly spiritual wisdom leads to holiness. Holiness is walking through life with God. Its fruit is increasing acquaintance with God.

- God gloriously empowers us for joyful endurance rather than for an escape from hardships.

- If we are in Christ, we are already in the kingdom, where Jesus is supreme, and we are already enjoying the firstfruits of an inheritance that is yet to come in its fullness.

- Jesus is supreme in relation to creation: He made it, and it subsists by His power and grace.

- God would have Jesus to have preeminence in the church.

- The Son is fully God who wonderfully became man and shed His blood to secure salvation. The measure of our salvation is the measure of His glory.

- We are called upon to continue firm in the contents of the Faith.

- Our prayers and longings should be fundamentally taken up with heavenly, spiritual realities.

Let's Pray

Amazing, glorious God,

we are breathless as we contemplate the wonders

of Your Son, our Savior,

and of what He has done for us.

We are amazed at His humanity,

amazed by His sacrifice,

and amazed by the power and fullness

of the salvation He secured.

We want Jesus to be preeminent in all we do

and, above all,

to seek those things that pertain to our walk with You.

Forgive us for our paltry views of Him,

and teach us to love and worship Him

more fully in the course of our lives

and as we gather as a congregation,

in His glorious name, amen.

Questions for Discussion and Study

1. Discuss the content of God's will as revealed in this passage.

2. Discuss God's empowerment as described in this passage. What is its measure and its purpose? What must we correct in the assumptions we held until now?

3. Summarize the nature of Jesus' realtionship to the Father, to creation, in salvation, and in eschatology.

4. Summarize what you have learned from this passage about man's need of salvation and the nature and extent of the salvation secured by Christ.

CHAPTER 3

The Mystery
(COLOSSIANS 1:24–29)

24 Now, I am thrilled with my sufferings for you and with filling up in my body what is lacking in the sufferings of the Christ for the sake of His body, which is the church, 25 of which I have become a servant in accordance with the responsibility God has given me for you to accomplish the Word of God, 26 the mystery that had been hidden from the beginning of the ages and from generations past but has now been shown to His consecrated ones 27 to whom God wanted to make known what are the riches of the glory of this mystery among the nations. That mystery is Christ among you, the hope for the glory, 28 whom we proclaim, warning every person and teaching every person with a full measure of wisdom 29 so we can present every person mature in Christ, for which I wrestle strenuously through the activity of Him who is powerfully active in me.

The opening word, *now*, introduces a new turn in the letter. Having described his prayer for the Colossians, Paul went on to describe his response to the gospel, and at the same time described his relations to his readers and intimated something of the grounds on which he wrote to them.

"I am thrilled with my sufferings for you and with filling up in my body what is lacking in the sufferings of the Christ for the sake of His body, which is the church." Paul was no masochist. He did not enjoy pain for pain's sake. Neither did he flee pain if it meant betraying his calling, obscuring the glory of Christ, or disadvantaging the churches of Christ. It was not the pain itself with which he was thrilled but the privilege of serving the church, even if it meant he had to suffer.

What steeled his heart and kept him going, ever onward, ever farther for the spread of the gospel, was the knowledge that his suffering served God. Paul did not view himself as a victim of circumstances. While in no way making light of the malice or reducing the responsibility of those who opposed him, he knew they too were instruments in God's hand, and that God would use his suffering for the good of the church.

Paul knew his pain benefited the church in an important way, and so he described his suffering as "filling up in my body what is lacking in the sufferings of the Christ for the sake of His body, which is the church." What did the apostle mean by this strange turn of phrase? Obviously Jesus' sacrificial death needs no supplementing, nor can any human add to what the all-sufficient Christ has achieved. In light of what Paul wrote above, that much should be clear. It will become clearer as we read on (2:6–15; 3:1–4). We must, therefore, concede Paul did not mean that Jesus came short of obtaining full salvation for those for whom He died, which salvation includes their sanctification and which is nothing less than their glorification, their transformation into the image of Christ (Romans 8:28–32; see Colossians 3:10). If their salvation was secured, what could Paul have meant by his statement?

Perhaps, if we give some thought to what he suffered on behalf of the church, we might find the answer. His sufferings were of two kinds. He suffered physically as he endured the hardships of his travels and the persecutions that resulted from his evangelistic endeavors. He described these in 2 Corinthians 11:23–37, where he spoke of "labors, imprisonment, countless beatings" and often being "near death." He then explicated:

Five times I received at the hands of the Jews the forty lashes less one. Three times I was beaten with rods. Once I was stoned. Three times I was shipwrecked; a night and a day I was adrift at sea; on frequent journeys, in danger from rivers, danger from robbers, danger from my own people, danger from Gentiles, danger in the city, danger in the wilderness, danger at sea, danger from false brothers; in toil and hardship, through many a sleepless night, in hunger and thirst, often without food, in cold and exposure.

He refused to satisfy the natural desire to have a wife (1 Corinthians 9:5), a settled life, and material security. Instead, where he could he worked for his own keep (1 Corinthians 9:6-19; 1 Thessalonians 2:9; 2 Thessalonians 3:8) while laboring in the gospel.

However, I suspect Paul would tell us these were not his primary sufferings. For the sake of the gospel, Paul experienced rejection both from his beloved nation and from fellow believers. To get a sense of Paul's love for his people, one need only to note what Paul wrote in Romans 9:1-3: "I am speaking the truth in Christ—I am not lying; my conscience bears me witness in the Holy Spirit—that I have great sorrow and unceasing anguish in my heart. For I could wish that I myself were accursed and cut off from Christ for the sake of my brothers, my kinsmen according to the flesh." Yet they thought him to be a troublemaker, a defiler of the temple, and an opponent of Moses and the Law. All because of his commitment to proclaim the gospel to all, Jew and Gentile alike, and to calling them to nothing more than faith in Christ and a life in accord with that Faith.

Even among his fellow believers Paul was often viewed with a measure of suspicion (Acts 21:17-21, 27-29). On one occasion (Galatians 2:11-21) he was forced to take public issue with Peter. Many times he had to defend the integrity of his calling and of the gospel he preached (Acts 13:44-46; 15:1-2; 17:3-7; 18:5-6, 12-13; 21:17-25; 22:1-22; 23:1-3; 24:1-21; 26:1-23; 2 Corinthians 1:12-4:18; 10:1-12:10; Galatians 1:10-2:10).

Think of it: instead of being encouraged by the nation to whom God had committed his Word, Paul was rejected and viewed as his nation's enemy for proclaiming that word. Instead of being encouraged by the apostles and his fellow believers, his steps were dogged by those who sought to modify his gospel, sway his converts and besmirch his name. Even when he arrived in Jerusalem, bearing gifts from the churches he established, he was called upon to demonstrate the falsity of the accusations made against him by publically following Jewish custom. Remember, he was arrested in Jerusalem and later transferred to Rome for one reason: he insisted on the equality of Jews and Gentiles in Christ, and on the freedom of both in Christ from the Law and from Jewish tradition.

On the surface, there was a good deal of logic behind the contentions of his fellow Jews as well as those of his fellow Christians who disagreed with him: The Old Testament, a distinctly Jewish book of religion, was the foundation of Paul's gospel. That Old Testament contained laws, and Jewish tradition (tradition was a much revered term in those days) claimed to faithfully interpret them. How could one be faithful to Christ without being faithful to the Law, and how could one be faithful to the Law without taking into account Jewish tradition, particularly pharisaic tradition? How could Paul claim to be faithful to the Law and in the same breath insist that Jews and Gentiles are not obliged to keep the Law?

But Paul could not and would not back down. He understood more clearly than some of his apostolic peers that grace spelled the end of all law-keeping for righteousness, as much as it spelled the destruction of the hoary division between Jews and Gentiles. They were one in sin, one in guilt, one in lostness and one as the objects of grace apart from any consideration but Christ's work on the cross. To divide the church was to deny grace as the foundation of one's standing before God; it was to lay a wholly different foundation. To divide the church was to deny the sufficiency of grace and therefore the sufficiency of the work of Christ. Such denials were never an option in Paul's mind, any more than they should be in ours. That is what Paul suffered for more than anything else.

There was another source of pain in Paul's life that he also embraced gladly. He made some reference to this source in 1:28–2:5, which we shall soon study. After describing his pains in 2 Corinthians 11, Paul added, "Apart from other things, there is the daily pressure on me of my anxiety for all the churches. Who is weak, and I am not weak? Who is made to fall, and I am not indignant?" (vv. 28–29). Paul was a caring individual, a true shepherd. The burden of caring for the churches, as can be seen from his letters, was a heavy burden indeed. True, he left most of the churches very soon after they were founded, but he continued to instruct them, care for them, and correct and challenge them to the day he died.

In these pains, Paul said, he rejoiced. He did so because he was suffering for the churches and for the churches' individual members. In so doing he was "filling up in his body what is lacking in the sufferings of the Christ for the sake of His body, which is the church." He followed in the footsteps of his Master, living out the gospel by denying himself and taking up the cross daily. He demonstrated that some things are worthy of sacrifice, that life is not a pleasure cruise, and that God in Christ must always come first. In the apostle's mind, putting God first meant according the church high priority, far before comfort, security, health, or even life itself.

Paul had become "a servant" of the church. God made him such ("in accordance with the responsibility God has given me for you"). For that reason, it was his duty "to accomplish the Word of God," to live it out and to proclaim it far and wide, so that the people of God would be gathered out of every tongue, tribe, and nation, united by the gospel, live for

Him as a body, and increasingly realize the wonders of His loving righteousness in the course of their shared lives.

The Word of God to be accomplished is "the mystery that had been hidden from the beginning of the ages and from generations past but has now been shown to His consecrated ones to whom God wanted to make known what are the riches of the glory of this mystery among the nations. That mystery is Christ among you, the hope for the glory." For clarity, let's abbreviate this long sentence before we consider its particulars. The mystery, once hidden and now revealed, has to do with "the riches of the glory ... among the nations."

That little word, *among*, is key. I greatly hesitate to go against the grain of common scholarly opinion. I make no claims to scholarly knowledge, but I believe it probable that the common way this Greek word, *en*, is translated in this context is incorrect. Paul did not, at this stage, have individual Christians in mind (he will in a moment) but the church as a whole, Christians as a collective. The "you" of this passage is "you Gentiles," and the *en* is not Christ dwelling in the heart of each individual, but dwelling in the church among the Gentiles, among whom he was not expected to dwell until the gospel proclaimed otherwise. That is the mystery for which Paul suffered (remember why he was arrested and under detention). That is what evokes "the hope for the glory."

If such a tremendous change had become reality, then surely it would be the harbinger and the assurance of something much greater. *En* is translated as I have translated it here, "among", in Matthew 2:6 ("among the princes"), for example, and in Matthew 3:23; 11:11; Luke 1:1, 25; 2:44; John 7:12; 11:54; Romans 1:2, 5, 6; 2:24; 11:17; Ephesians 1:18; 3:8; 5:3; Philippians 2:15; Colossians 1:6; 3:11; and many other places.

For still further clarity, let us look for a moment at the parallel passage in Ephesians 3:4-6 (ESV), where Paul spoke of "the mystery of Christ, which was not made known to the sons of men in other generations as it has now been revealed to His holy apostles and prophets by the Spirit. This mystery is that the Gentiles are fellow heirs, members of the same body, and partakers of the promise in Christ Jesus through the gospel."

The mystery Paul served, for which he suffered and which loomed so large in the apostle's mind, was exactly that: the unity of the church on the grounds of grace as an indication of the sufficiency of Christ's work and the finality of His accomplishments. God is to be gloried through His grace; a grace that unites Jews and Gentiles, slaves and freemen, men and women into one body; a grace that demands of them to live together and then equips them to that end.

Now let's return to the particulars of the passage. This mystery, Paul told the Colossians, "had been hidden from the beginning of the ages and from generations past." Please note, this does not mean the mystery was wholly unknown. It simply means that it was not as clearly known in the past because it was not as clearly revealed and therefore known as it is since Christ came.

Grace was always the grounds of a relationship with God. Abraham did nothing to merit God's call; any good he did was the fruit of that call. That is true of Moses and of the Judges, of Samuel and of David. Nowhere in Scripture do we find a case in which God responded to man's faith or faithfulness by calling him to Himself. Quite to the contrary. We find men, even after their call, failing yet forgiven and sustained. The initiative is always God's. The gospel of grace is to be found in the Old Testament history and law. It is just not as clearly declared.

What is more, we find that unity between all men under God is not a New Testament invention. Biblical history begins with the history of the world, not with the call of Abraham. God had the world in mind when He called Abraham (Genesis 12:3), and throughout the course of the biblical narrative we meet non-Israelites who loved and served the Lord, including Ruth and Naaman. Recall the mixed multitude brought out of Egypt (Exodus 12: 38) and into covenant at Sinai, and the repeated biblical insistence that Israel's God is to be acknowledged by all nations. The Old Testament eschatological expectation is described in Malachi 1:11 as inclusive of the Gentiles: "From the rising of the sun to its setting my name will be great among the nations, and in every place incense will be offered to my name, and a pure offering. For my name will be great among the nations, says the LORD of hosts." The Psalms are replete with such an expectation:

> The LORD looks down from heaven on the children of man, to see if there are any who understand, who seek after God (14:2).

> The heavens declare the glory of God, and the sky above proclaims His handiwork. Day to day pours out speech, and night to night reveals knowledge. There is no speech, nor are there words, whose voice is not heard. Their voice goes out through all the earth, and their words to the end of the world (19:1–4).

The earth is the LORD's and the fullness thereof, the world and those who dwell therein (24:1).

Let all the earth fear the LORD; let all the inhabitants of the world stand in awe of Him (33:8).

Sing praises to God, sing praises! Sing praises to our King, sing praises! For God is the King of all the earth; sing praises with a psalm! God reigns over the nations; God sits on His holy throne. The princes of the peoples gather as the people of the God of Abraham (47:6–9).

And, of course:

Why do the nations rage and the peoples plot in vain? The kings of the earth set themselves, and the rulers take counsel together, against the LORD and against his Anointed, saying, "Let us burst their bonds apart and cast away their cords from us." He who sits in the heavens laughs; the Lord holds them in derision. Then He will speak to them in His wrath, and terrify them in His fury, saying, "As for Me, I have set My King on Zion, My holy hill." I will tell of the decree: The LORD said to me, "You are My Son; today I have begotten You. Ask of Me, and I will make the nations Your heritage, and the ends of the earth Your possession (2:1–9).

And:

May God be gracious to us and bless us and make His face to shine upon us, Selah that Your way may be known on earth, Your saving power among all nations. Let the peoples praise You, O God; let all the peoples praise You! Let the nations be glad and sing for joy, for You judge the peoples with equity and guide the nations upon earth. Selah Let the peoples praise You, O God; let all the peoples praise You (67:1–5).

Israelite identity is never shown in the Old Testament to be the grounds of God's favor any more than in the New. The gospel of grace is found in the Old Testament history and law. It is not as pronounced but, in fact, is found repeatedly. God called Abraham out of the blue, at His own initiative, and He forgave Abraham repeatedly. Isaac and Jacob were chosen before they were born. David committed heinous sins, yet found forgiveness after the Lord brought him to repentance (Psa. 32). Judah repeatedly turned away from the Lord and was forgiven. Neither was any sign of repentance shown before the people were allowed to return from Babylon in Ezra and Nehemiah's time. In fact, the returned was promised even before the people were exiled. Israel did not seek a means of atonement but it was unilaterally provided.

The principle of grace was there, but hidden. Paul did not attribute its hiddenness to the nature of the mystery, nor did he associate it with past generations' hardness of heart, unworthiness, or anything else that might have to do with them. Rather, the truth was hidden from Israel by a unilateral act of God (Isaiah 6:10, 44:18). Paul certainly did not describe the mystery as God's response to reality (such as Israel's rejection of the gospel, as some would have us believe). It existed "from the beginning of the ages" for reasons divine majesty has not chosen to disclose and as a sovereign act of him whose prerogative it is to hide or to reveal matters.

"But now," in the coming of Christ and the preaching and living of the gospel by those faithful to Christ, the mystery "has been shown to His consecrated ones." The revelation has not come to all, but it has come to all who are the Lord's, including the Colossian Christians (Colossians 1:1). No elite within the church was the recipient of this revelation; it was the happy possession of all who are in Christ. Paul challenged the preposterous claim made by the Colossian false teachers that there were among the redeemed some to whom more revelation is given than others.

"To whom God wanted to make known." John Calvin's remarks here say it all:

> Here [Paul] puts a bridle on the boldness of men, that they may not let themselves be wiser or more inquisitive than they should, but may learn to be satisfied with this one thing, that it has so pleased God. For the will of God ought to be perfectly sufficient for us as a reason. This, however, is said principally to commend the grace of God. For Paul suggests that men by no means provided any cause for God's making them participants of this secret, when he teaches that He was led to this of His own accord, and because he *willed so*. For it is customary for Paul to oppose the good pleasure of God to all human merits and external causes.

God wanted all the consecrated ones to know "what are the riches of the glory of this mystery among the nations." There are riches of grace and of glory to be found in living together in a church, especially when those who would not naturally choose to live together find a common bond, a common goal, and a common affection one for another because of the grace of God in Christ. Differences pale into insignificance because Christ outshines them all. The wonder of His person, the beauty of His gospel, the power of His presence and the marvelous reality of His grace surpass any racial, social, educational, political, or doctrinal differences. Christ becomes all in all. That is what he ought to be in the church. The church is a primary means by which God makes known "what are the riches of the glory of this mystery among the nations."

But there is more to it than that. What church life ought to be and can be in the here and now is but a whisper of the wonders of what will be in the future, a deposit of the glory that is to come. As Paul put it, living together in church, Jews and Gentiles, slaves, slave owners and freemen, Scythians, barbarians, and the cultured, gives added rise to "the hope for the glory." Church life, when properly conducted, when Christ is first and grace is the foundation, evokes and sustains an amazing, energizing, thrilling hope for the glory. Note the definite article. Paul did not speak of a hope for glory in general but of a specifically directed hope for a very specific glory: the glory of being in Christ, the glory of Christ Himself, the exaltation of God through grace through all generations, heaven accomplished and enjoyed!

That is the product of what Paul described as "Christ among you." Just as the Colossians were commended for their all-inclusive love in which there was no distinction, so did Paul labor inclusively for all, and so he called upon the church to labor. "Christ among you" means He is to be among you as you conduct church, among you as you relate to one another, among you—Jews and Gentiles—united in one body, among you in terms of the hope that energizes you in the daily walk of life with one another.

That is what church is all about. That is also why Paul was so taken up with Jesus. The apostle's gospel could be summed up in that one title— the Christ—and in that one perception— "Christ among you"—because every aspect of the gospel issues out of Him, hangs on Him, and returns to Him. To preach the gospel is to preach Christ. To know the gospel is more than knowing a series of truths. It is to have a personal acquaintance with God in Christ and in the company of others who are different from you.

"Whom we proclaim," said Paul, "warning every person," Jew or Gentile, pleasant or difficult, wise or foolish, slave or master, male or female, black or white, Charismatic or Reformed, Baptist or Presbyterian. Paul loved all of God's consecrated ones and labored to ensure every person among them continued in Christ and was subject to Him in every way. To that end he and they had to be focused on Christ.

Paul continued to describe his strenuous efforts on the part of every individual in Christ by pointing at the means he used: "teaching every person with a full measure of wisdom," carefully, gently, persistently, taking into account their ability to understand and realizing that such an ability has to do with more than just intellectual comprehension, "so we can present every person mature in Christ." That is one of the most important functions of a church, the major part of every service. A church that focuses on anything else is off focus. A church that measures growth in numerical terms rather than in the cultivation among its members of an informed, affectionate, day-to-day commitment to Christ and the pursuit of holiness, has adopted an unbiblical measure. Paul strove to reach every person by way of instruction.

He does not tire in this letter of the phrase *every person*. His repeated use of those words shows how much he wanted to drive this message home. All, without distinction, are to be the object of gospel mercies. For that reason, every individual is to be the recipient of love and instruction. The spiritual health of every person in Christ should be the object of our sincere and loving effort as it was of Paul's.

Are there lonely people in your church? Are people suffering—or rejoicing—having no one with whom to share their thoughts and feelings? How lonely is your pastor or his wife? Are single parents forced to cope with life without a helping hand? Are young couples learning to live together with no one to guide and encourage them? Is someone struggling with sin, or sickness, or any other kind of difficulty, alone in the wilderness of his pain? Is there a young person who needs mentoring or an older person you can visit? Are there newcomers you can welcome? When did you last write the church's missionary, show interest in his wife, send a parcel for his children?

The goal is the maturity of each individual for the welfare of the whole. No church is healthier than its weakest member. The commonly applied selective process by which churches today rid themselves of the more difficult people, of those who differ, of the unkind, the immature, and the unwise, is contrary to the standard Paul presented. Churches should care—sincerely and sacrificially—for every individual who lays legitimate claim to saving faith in Christ. Sometimes such caring will include the need for firm and loving discipline. Whatever it takes, we should exert ourselves, like Paul, for every person. The fact that churches take on a social status and, in the course of time, are welcoming but to a certain class of people, is plain wrong because it is unbiblical. The New Testament church was made up of all kinds. The kind of thinking that is behind the modern "people's movements" is contra-biblical, however terse an anthropological argument you might wish to make. The gospel runs against the stream of human preferences. It insists of seating slaves and slave-owners on the same bench, Jews and Gentiles, Blacks and Caucasians. It creates a different kind of society, a heavenly one; the church as a means of sanctification, leading on to glory.

Paul's description of his efforts is quite striking. He proclaimed a warning, utilizing every ounce of wisdom he could muster to drive that warning home. This was a public act, and it should characterize preaching today. A preacher's call is not to comfort people in their sins but to call them away from their sins to the sacred comforts of the gospel. Paul preached and taught, with a focus on every individual. This can be done both publicly and privately. Both activities were not only accompanied "with a full measure of wisdom," but were conducted by way of strenuous wrestling. The term Paul used indicates a kind of agonizing struggle, a wrestling match, in which contestants lay hold of each other in close proximity, feel each other's body heat, smell each other's perspiration, and exert themselves maximally, seeking a moment of opportunity to win the match. Paul engaged with each individual to an extent and in a spirit that could only be described in terms of such close proximity, such strenuous exertions. What a picture of pastoral concern.

Paul was very much aware of the fact that he could do nothing of spiritual value apart from God, and that any spiritual good he achieved was the product of God working through him. Once again we experience the biblical tension between man's endeavors and God's overruling power. Paul's efforts were nothing less than "the activity of Him who [was] powerfully active in" him. Paul consciously, intentionally, freely exerted himself, and God was powerfully active in him to do all according to His divine good pleasure.

Let's Summarize

- Paul delighted to suffer for the church because he knew the church is the means by which God is going to glorify His Son. Loving Christ, Paul could not help but love the church and follow his Lord in suffering for it.

- The work of Christ is perfect. It meets every need to perfection, which is why it cannot be supplemented.

- The church is a means God uses to glorify us by way of sanctification.

- To divide the church is to deny the gospel.

- God has now revealed what was a hidden mystery: Christ is among the Gentiles. Jews and Gentiles join together, a harbinger of glory to come, a taste of heaven on earth, of the future in the present.

- God uses the church to reveal the riches of His glory: Jews and Gentiles, loving God and each other, respecting each other, and serving God as one body in which there is no difference.

- An expansive view of the church does not come at the expense of recognizing the value of individuals. Paul labored for the church at large and for individuals in particular, seeking to apply wisdom in the application of the gospel to each in the varying circumstances of their lives.

Let's Pray

Great God and Father of us all,

Your eternal plan is stupendous, glorious, beyond imagination:

What sin and pride have separated, You bring together.

The walls that human arrogance have constructed, You destroy.

We recognize with gratitude

the wonder of church as it ought to be

and confess that our church life

is not a manifestation of Your glory as it ought to be.

We recognize the beauty of loving others for Christ's sake

and beg Your forgiveness for rejecting them

because they were not like us.

We confess the arrogance

of considering ourselves better than others

and seek Your mercy

as we labor to love them as we love ourselves

so that our conduct will manifest the mystery hidden for ages

and now revealed through the church.

Cleanse us, Lord,

and teach us the humility

that is necessary for us to honor You.

In the name of Your Son, our Savior,

Jesus the Christ, amen.

QUESTIONS FOR DISCUSSION AND STUDY:

1. Show from Old Testament passages not quoted above that salvation is by grace.

2. Summarize what Paul said in his letter to the Colossians about the glory of God. Compare your findings with his letters to the Romans and the Ephesians.

3. What would you consider to be the main source of pain in Paul's life and how did he cope with it according to this passage?

4. Are there modern parallels to the insistence on the authority of tradition that the early church faced? What is the basis of such a mistaken insistence and what is its biblical resolution?

CHAPTER 4

Live Out the Gospel
(COLOSSIANS 2:1–12)

1 Because of which I want you to know how great a struggle I have on your behalf, on behalf of those in Laodicea and of everyone who has not personally met me, 2 so that their hearts may be comforted, their being linked together by love and leading to all the riches of a full assurance of understanding, leading in turn to full knowledge of God's mystery—Christ— 3 in whom are hidden all the treasures of wisdom and knowledge. 4 I say this so that no one will mislead you with persuasive talk 5 because, if I am actually bodily absent still, in the spirit, I am with you and am rejoicing, seeing the orderliness and steadiness of your faith in Christ.

6 Because of that, as you have received the Christ, Jesus the Lord, in Him conduct yourselves, 7 having been rooted and being constructed in Him and confirmed in the Faith as you were taught, overflowing in giving thanks. 8 Be alert so that there is no one who is robbing you by way of philosophy and empty deceit that is compatible with human traditions, with the basic elements of the world, and incompatible with Christ, 9 because in Him—bodily—all the fullness of the Godhead dwells 10 and you have been filled in Him, who is the head of all rule and authority, 11 in whom you were also circumcised with a circumcision not performed by hands, by the removal of the fleshly body by the circumcision Christ performs: 12 co-buried with Him in the bap-

tism, in whom you were also co-raised through faith in the work of God—the raising of Him (Jesus) from the dead.

It is unfortunate that some translations omit Paul's opening phrase, "because of which," that connects what is about to be said with what was said in verse 28. Connecting words serve an important purpose, and translations provide a disservice when they are omitted.

In 1:28, Paul spoke of the content of his preaching and the nature of his efforts on behalf of the Colossians. He wants them to be aware of these, and to be both encouraged and challenged by them to strive with the same goals in mind. Paul was seeking to enlist the Colossians' cooperation. To that end, he goes on to say, "I want you to know how great a struggle I have on your behalf." He refers to his struggle in verses 28–29 of the previous chapter, when he described his efforts on behalf of each one of them, to "present every person mature in Christ." Here he continues with the same theme.

His struggle is conducted not only on behalf of the Colossians but also "on behalf of those in Laodicea and of everyone who has not personally met me." As noted in the introduction, Laodicea was not far from Colossae, and the churches in both cities were probably founded through Epaphras' efforts. Paul had no part in their founding and had never visited these churches before he composed this letter.

The apostle now describes again the purpose to which he exerted himself so strenuously: to the end that "their hearts may be comforted, their being linked together by love and leading to all the riches that belong to a full assurance of understanding, leading in turn to full knowledge of God's mystery—Christ—in whom are hidden all the treasures of wisdom and knowledge."

Of course we will want to unpack this wonderfully rich statement, but we need to look at it first as a whole. Having read as far as we have in this letter, it is not surprising to discover Paul's concern was for unity in the church. Nor is it surprising to note this unity leads to spiritual growth, particularly to spiritual perception. The apostle has already said as much.

Here Paul once again enlists terminology characteristic to the false teachers, who promised their adherents a close bond of comradeship and a fuller understanding that would allow them to reach perfection through mysteries others were unable to comprehend. Comfort and understanding, Paul insists, are to be found in Christ and in the company of all God's consecrated ones, nowhere else.

Paul wants their hearts to "be comforted." It is possible the apostle is referring to a specific circumstance the Colossian Christians had to face, of which we know nothing. It is also possible Paul is simply referring to the realities of human life in community, particularly such as are familiar to us from the book of Acts and from his other writings, and to which we have already made reference. A mixed community of Jews and Gentiles, slaves and freemen, people from various social strata in the highly strati-fied Roman society would have inevitably accentuated tensions that are always involved with imperfect people living together. Of course, a com-bination of the two is also possible.

On the other hand, he may be speaking of the sweet comfort that comes from being united in affectionate, supportive fellowship. Man was made for community. He is never healthy when lacking the give and take, the embrace and challenge involved in living in the company of others. Modern-day individualism, with its virtual communities, so amenable to manipulation and so unlike real human camaraderie, has lost sight of the value of real community. Our nuclear families, single-parent homes, TV children, smartphone and tablet kids, smilies, Whatsapp and Facebook so-called "friends" are in danger of losing the art of interpersonal com-munication and are a far cry from true human community. Churches and families in Christ need to recapture this vision and call society back to its moorings. They need to cultivate a biblical understanding and practice of community.

Paul was engaged in a struggle for the Colossians' comfort and en-couragement. He wanted them to experience the richness of church life rather than withdraw into a purportedly elite ghetto such as the heretics were seeking to establish. Their comfort had to do with being "linked together by love," a love that (as he reminded the Corinthians in 1 Corin-thians 13 under similar circumstances) does not vaunt itself over others nor seek to compete with them; it labors for their welfare. Love draws people together and Christians are to love all men, especially those who belong to the household of faith, regardless of any other factors.

The concept of a linkage between Christians is very apropos. There is no merging. Jews do not cease to be Jews, freemen to be freemen, or women to be women. Every link maintains its distinct identity, while each is firmly connected to another. Love is the connection. If we loved more, we would argue less, criticize less, and give more of ourselves. If we loved more sincerely, churches would not split, pastors would not be run off of their turf, and individual congregants would not be neglected. All would grow together in grace and in the knowledge of God.

Such loving linkage serves important purposes:

1. It leads "to all the riches of a full assurance of understanding." Many truths can only be understood properly in the context of church life, simply because church life is about loving God in Christ, and loving God in Christ is about church life. One simply cannot consistently be a Christian without belonging to a congregation, sharing in its life, contributing to its welfare, partnering in its worship, growing in its context, and submitting to its discipline.

When knowledge has been tried and proven, when it is transformed from intellectual knowledge to knowledge that comes from experience, it congeals into the kind of mature, humble, and gracious confidence Paul here describes as "the full assurance of understanding." We know the power of the gospel because we have experienced it. We know the truth of Scripture because we have tried it out and found it to be true. We know the grace of God because we experience it every day of our lives. We understand as never before.

2. Such assurance leads to still further understanding and, when speaking of church life, it leads "to full knowledge of God's mystery—Christ—in whom are hidden all the treasures of wisdom and knowledge." Paul had described the mystery earlier in terms of the unity between Jew and Gentile. Here he describes it as Christ Himself. The reason for that is that Christ is known in the church as He can be known nowhere else. He is known when we experience His presence in each other and in the transforming power of His grace as we reach across the barriers that normally divide people.

If we had any doubt that Paul was responding to the false teaching being promulgated in Colossae, he sets our minds at ease by clearly stating, "I say this so that no one will mislead you with persuasive talk." Obviously some were seeking to mislead them. Whether they succeeded is open to question, but Paul clearly identified a danger in the verbal abilities of the heretics. People tend to be impressed by talent. They are more easily swayed by oratory than by content.

In these days of slogans, sound bites and superficial thinking, when culture is more influenced by what it sees on television than what it hears in church, the danger is all the greater. We should tune our hearts to our minds, and our minds to testing words, sentences, and whole messages against God's Word if we wish to protect ourselves from bad influences. It is not without reason Jesus' primary activity, like that of the prophets, was teaching rather than miracle working. For the same reason God gave us His revelation in words rather than pictures.

The Faith of the Bible is a Faith that demands, encourages, and enhances thinking. It motivates and guides believers to seek the internal logic of the universe. Science, history, and art take on eternal meaning. Language and culture are not viewed as the fruit of happenstance but as, in some sense, a work of God, or a corruption of that work. Their inner workings have meaning, and understanding those workings is part of man's duty before God. Commenting on this verse in his commentary on Colossians, John Calvin reminded us:

> Since many, content with a slight taste, have nothing but a confused and fitful knowledge, [Paul] mentions expressly the *riches of understanding* (Italics in the original). By this phrase he means full and clear perception. And at the same time he admonishes them that, according to the measure of understanding, they must make progress in love.

Still addressing the danger of the Colossians being turned from the path of the gospel to a false message, Paul adds by way of encouragement, "Because, if I am actually bodily absent still ["absent" because, to the time of writing, Paul had not been able to visit the Colossian church], in the spirit I am with you [Paul was not laying claim to a mystical presence; he was simply saying that he cared about the Colossians and was informed of their welfare] and am rejoicing [obviously, at least a good portion of the church rejected the heretical teaching], seeing the orderliness and steadiness of your faith in Christ."

The latter are military terms. *Orderliness* refers to soldiers establishing camp or maintaining ranks as they march. *Steadiness* refers to soldiers maintaining a solid front in the face of an attack. The Colossian Christians were engaged in a spiritual battle and maintained good order. They refused to retreat before the persuasive speech of the heretics. Instead, they maintained their resistance and held a common front.

By commending the believers in such terms, Paul is encouraging them to be all he said they were. The apostle knew how to encourage people to do well. There were times when it was necessary to criticize and rebuke. However much Paul did not enjoy it, he did not shirk the duty when there was no better way. But he always preferred to address churches and individuals positively. His letter to Philemon, written at the same time and delivered with the letter to the Colossians, is a superb example of such gracious wisdom.

"Because of that, as you have received the Christ, Jesus the Lord, in Him conduct yourselves." Paul continued his appeal. Since they had carried themselves so well up to this point, Paul exhorted them to continue. At the same time, he called them back to Christ: "As you have received the Christ, Jesus the Lord, in Him conduct yourselves." Such an exhortation ran directly contrary to the teaching he was challenging, that called upon the Colossians to progress beyond what they had received in Christ. Paul is saying (and will say it clearer as he proceeds) that there is nothing beyond Christ. The best step the Colossians could take on their way to spirituality was to return to Christ as they had originally received Him.

It is amazing—and deeply disappointing—to note how relevant such a call is for the church today. All kinds of gimmicks, doctrines, and methods are adopted instead of the simple, but by no means simplistic, faith in the power of God through the work of the Spirit on the grounds of the work of Christ. Empowerment, enlightenment, spiritual gifts, seeker-friendliness, contemporary or traditional worship, evangelism, children's programs, miracles, love for Israel, Jewish tradition, Jewish roots, family-oriented ... you name it: everything but Jesus. Surely Christian churches ought to be known above all in relation to Christ!

We allow the world to shape us, to determine our emphases. Somehow we do not understand that Christ is sufficient. We think His work needs to be supplemented. It needs to be rendered more relevant, more appealing. That is the false logic behind so many of the seeker-sensitive churches today, much of what purports today to be worship is really nothing more than entertainment. Paul entertained no such thoughts. He was Christ-oriented and fully persuaded that Christ is all we need. He believed Jesus was eminently relevant and gloriously attractive, so he calls the Colossians back to Christ with no additions. They were to conduct their private and congregation life in Him, and in Him alone.

Paul says their future should be consistent with their past, "having been rooted [past tense] and being constructed [present continuous] in Him and confirmed in the Faith as you were taught [past tense], overflowing in giving thanks [present continuous]." They had been rooted by Epaphras in Christ as trees are rooted in the ground, and were now "being constructed" and "confirmed" in Him by their teachers as buildings are constructed, with solid foundations. Recognizing the value of what they had received and were receiving in Christ through their teachers, the Christians in Colossae were being encouraged to persist in pressing forward in Him rather than in seeking something more than Christ can offer.

For that purpose, they needed to "be alert." Paul is speaking of a spiritually motivated, biblically guided intellectual alertness that tests what is said and can identify doctrinal errors, both overt and incipient, because it is equipped with the information necessary for proper evaluation. Being a Christian involves thinking. Growing in Christ includes growth in understanding. What we believe, how we think, and the doctrines we embrace impact our spiritual lives for good or for ill. That is why Paul warned against "philosophy and empty deceit."

He is not saying that as such philosophy is wrong or in any way contrary to the Christian faith. After all, philosophy is but another name for theology—how we look at life, how we perceive God, what we think is the purpose of all things. But philosophy (like theology) can also be a vehicle that will take us where we do not, certainly ought not, want to go. The difference between philosophy and theology is their basis. Theology learns from God through the Scriptures; philosophy tries to understand the world by its own means. But they both result in a perspective of reality that shapes our lives.

Paul referred to philosophy because so-called lovers of wisdom (which is what the Greek term originally meant) were popular in the Greek and Roman cultures. Purported philosophers traveled throughout the Empire peddling their philosophical teachings. The Colossian heretics obviously presented themselves as those who loved and represented a spiritual kind of philosophy. But this was "empty deceit." They loved not the truth but the sense of being its possessors, with the sense of importance and the powers of influence that generally accompany it.

Paul warns the Christians in Colossae to be alert "so that there is no one who is robbing you by way of philosophy and empty deceit." They were to be intellectually alert so as to be able to detect if someone was trying rob them. Rob them? What is Paul talking about? The doctrines that gave Paul reason for concern were offered as a means of enrichment or spiritual advance, not robbery.

That is exactly Paul's point: the promulgators of the new teaching promised spiritual enrichment. Their doctrines were capable of delivering an initial rush of what was thought to be a heightened spiritual experience. But once the novelty faded, instead of being enriched, adherents were impoverished; instead of more of God, they had less. They were starved by malnutrition and endless striving that sapped their spiritual strength. Increasingly, their worship became the product of emotional manipulation rather than of a vivid comprehension of God's holiness and grace as the products of good teaching. Their sense of security was eroded because they came to believe it all depended on them. Their satisfaction was replaced by an ever-increasing need of greater stimulation. Their moral sensitivity was dulled by constant failure.

Does this sound familiar? Have you been taken up by a false philosophy and empty deceit? Have you embarked on a search for more, only to find yourself with less? Then heed the apostle's advice and turn back to Christ as you first heard of Him when you were converted and brought into God's favor.

Tradition was a value in those days. The hoarier, the holier, it was thought. But a tradition that originated from the spiritual world, or purported to know spiritual secrets— now that was a tradition worth knowing. Again, Paul frames his terminology to counter the false teaching in Colossae. His readers are called to beware lest they be robbed by a philosophy masquerading in the form of a spiritual tradition. Such traditions, he insists, are merely human. They have to do with the lowest elements of reality rather than the higher. They can never be compared with Christ. As Paul puts it, they are "compatible with human traditions, with the basic elements of the world, and incompatible with Christ."

The term I've translated as "basic elements" was often used to refer to learning the alphabet. So Paul is saying that, rather than teaching a higher spirituality, the Colossian heretics were teaching the ABCs of the universe, the most basic, simplest matters from which they should have progressed long ago.

Rather than bringing the initiate into contact with the highest of the divine emanations, the doctrines and ceremonies of the heretics had to do with the "basic," basest "elements of the world." They were taken up with matters of food, drink, and ceremonial purity, rather than with what constitutes true holiness: a love for God that drives individuals to hunger for Him and to obey Him, a morality that has God's person and His law at its core, and God's pleasure and glory as its goal. That is what Christ teaches. Such is the only kind of spirituality that is compatible with Christ.

Christ is exactly opposite the base elements of the world. He is their Maker and they are made; He is non-contingent and they exist by virtue of His command; He is utter purity and they are contaminated by sin. They are inevitably "incompatible with Christ, because in Him— bodily—all the fullness of the Godhead dwells."

We've seen what the term *fullness* meant to the Colossian heresy. Paul is saying that every ounce of deity, every feature that may legitimately be associated with being God, every divine attribute, every divine power, every distinctively divine action belongs to Christ. It belonged to Him even before He took on a bodily existence and was known as Jesus the son of Mary, and it is to be found in Him now. There are no emanations; there is no demiurge. Jesus is God in the full sense of the term, and so remains (*dwells*, in the present tense, not "dwelt." Paul is describing an ongoing reality).

That being the case, there is no reason to look for anything beyond Him. Christ is all-sufficient. As long as Jesus remains the focus of our attention, the goal of our aspirations and the measure of everything we are invited to believe or practice, we have an excellent measuring rod by which to evaluate other things. The pretention to be able to add to what Christ has accomplished is, in fact, to deny His sufficiency and to diminish the glory of His perfect Godhood. After all, what can be better than knowing God manifest in the flesh, walking with Him in whom "all the fullness of the Godhead dwells"? What greater salvation can be imagined?

When Jesus became man, He did not cease to be God. His manhood hid His deity, restrained its manifestation, obscured its reality. But He was God manifest in the flesh. Very man of very man, very God of very God. Even as He sucked at His mother's breast or had His diaper changed, He upheld the world by His powerful Word. As He slept, He made the earth revolve around the sun and kept the stars in their place. At the same that time that He hung on the cross and was carried to the grave, He shared the throne of God and ruled the destinies of men. "All," not part, of the fullness dwelt in Him.

"And you have been filled in Him." The measure of Christ is the measure of our salvation because it is the measure of His accomplishments on our behalf. We are filled from His fullness. That is why a poor view of Christ leads inevitably to a poor view of the gospel. Paul dares use with regard to Christians the same Greek term (*filled*) he used with regard to Christ (*fullness*), although in a different sense because the redeemed are *filled* with His glorious *fullness*.

Who, then, needs more than Christ? What more could be had?

Paul next delves into particulars. Being God in all His glory, Jesus is inevitably "the head of all rule and authority." The terms rule and authority include both earthly and heavenly powers, real and imagined. The apostle puts Jesus above Caesar, above the angels, above all of the spiritual beings the heretics claimed to exist. What is more, since the heretics taught a combination of mysticism and Judaism (or of some Jewish practice), Paul goes on to say "in whom [that is, in Christ] you were also circumcised with a circumcision not performed by hands, by the removal of the fleshly body by the circumcision Christ performs." Circumcision was a sign of the covenant, evidence that an individual belonged to the people of God. As such, He was the chosen recipient of the blessing of the covenant.

Whatever Jewish custom offers, Jesus offers more (as the writer to the Hebrews put it, "better": Hebrews 6:9; 7:19, 22; 8:6; 9:23; 10:34; 11:16, 35, 40). Whatever Moses offers, Jesus offers more. After all, Moses was instrumental in giving Israel a law meant to bring the people to Christ. It was not complete in itself but pointed forward (the essence of the argument of the letter of the Hebrews). Nor was it an essential part of spiritual life—it was given many years after the creation of the world, many years after the call of Abraham, and it underwent changes when the people were about to enter the promised land after forty years of wandering. The Law was a shadow and Christ is the substance (Paul would shortly say as much). Now that Christ has come, law-keeping must no longer be seen as the means to know, love, and serve God. As much and more is true of Jewish tradition, described by Paul as "human traditions … incompatible with Christ."

Paul denies that such traditions have divine authority and are compatible with Christ. They have no place in the Christian life, none in our walk with God. The reason is, simply, that human inventions are no more than human inventions. They cannot convey spiritual realities. At best they can symbolize them, much like an idol cannot convey the presence or majesty of God, although it may well serve to express their maker's view of Him. That is one of the dangers involved in their use. They are expressions of man's comprehensions of God rather than of God as He is. However, the few simple ceremonies given by God (in our day, baptism and communion) are faithful expressions of God's self-revelation and are accompanied by the secret working of His Spirit.

Baptism is not a mere symbol. Nor is it exclusively an act conducted by a church and undergone by an individual. Accompanying the act is the work of the Spirit of God, transforming the ceremony into a sacrament, a means by which God draws near to bless, affirm, and edify His people. This is also true of communion.

If these symbols, given by God, can be misused and misinterpreted, what shall we say of human inventions, however ancient they may be? That is precisely why God forbade human accretions to His worship. The time, posture, and physical location of worship, the language employed and whether one uses a piano, an organ, or an orchestra, these and similar matters are incidental. But the actual content of worship, for example, whether we have preaching or a play, whether we pray or not—these have to do with the essence of worship and must be guided exclusively by the Word of God. Man has no right to intrude himself into these matters. He has no right to control how God is to be worshipped.

So much, then, for the Hebrew Roots and Messianic Movements. They are inevitably included under the category of "human traditions" and are, as such, "incompatible with Christ." Contrary to their claims, there is nothing to be had from God that cannot be found in Christ. Jewish traditions have no right to be considered of spiritual value in the worship of God. They add cultural setting and are relevant to those brought up in a Jewish culture, but they add nothing to our spirituality and contribute nothing to our walk with God.

Of Gentiles who came to faith in Christ, Paul says they "were" circumcised (he would not need to say this if they were Jewish). They did not need to be circumcised again. Their circumcision was "a circumcision not performed by human hands" which can remove no more than a foreskin, but a circumcision that involved "the removal of the fleshly body by the circumcision Christ performs." Choose, Paul is saying: Christ's circumcision or that performed by human hands. A physical circumcision or a spiritual one wrought by Him in whom the fullness of the Godhead dwells. How was this circumcision accomplished? By our being "co-buried with Him [with Christ] in the baptism [not just any baptism, but a distinctly Christian baptism; the definite article is not required by the Greek unless it serves a specific purpose], in whom you were also co-raised through faith in the work of God [which work Paul identified in the next phrase]—the raising of Him [Jesus] from the dead."

Of course, Paul does not intend to imply that baptism involves a physical death by which those baptized no longer live in the body. He is saying that baptism, far from being merely a symbol, affects something real in the life of the person being baptized. That reality is described as being "co-buried" and "co-raised" with Christ, a participation in the death, burial, and resurrection of Christ that becomes a reality in the course of baptism; an actual participation in the death and resurrection of Christ. Not regeneration, but something related to it. Not salvation, but something integral to it.

This does not happen automatically, by virtue of the ceremony. It happens "through faith in the work of God." Baptism has an effect through faith, which immediately implies that faith is necessary to baptism. Of course, the question may legitimately be asked: Whose faith? Since the only persons in view here are those who had been baptized, the natural conclusion is that their faith is in view. Candidates for baptism must have faith before being admitted to the sacrament. It is their faith, combined with the God-given ceremony conducted in accordance with the Word of God and the secret workings of the Spirit, that make baptism to be what it is.

Lightfoot put it well: "Baptism is the grave of the old man, and the birth of the new. As he sinks beneath the baptismal waters, the believer buries there all his corrupt affections and past sins; as he emerges thence, he rises regenerate, quickened to new hopes and a new life. This it is, because it is not only the crowning act of his own faith but also the seal of God's adoption and the earnest of God's Spirit. Thus baptism is an image of his participation both in the death and the resurrection of Christ."[11]

LET'S SUMMARIZE

- We must beware of persuasive words. The way to beware is to develop an understanding of the Faith through serious, systematic biblical and doctrinal studies. We need to be doctrinally alert because error robs us. Doctrines have great practical consequences.

- It is not easy to live in a church where people differ, but such is our calling. We will find comfort in loving others on the grounds of what Christ has done and the hope we share for the future. Love unites.

- Living as we ought in the church leads to further spiritual growth because we experience and, in this way, understand more of the

---

[11] Lightfoot, *Saint Paul's Epistles to the Colossians and Philemon*, 184.

truth than we can merely by theoretical knowledge. Such learning cultivates humble confidence in the truth, leading to still further understanding.

- There is nothing to be found of God beyond Christ. There should be no other focus in our church life. If there are any, we have become like the world by focusing on our differences instead of on Christ. Our trust should be wholly in Him, not in our efforts. We are complete in Him, circumcised in Him, dead and raised in Him. He is above all—above the angels, above Moses, above Abraham.

- There is no place for traditions beyond God's Word, not even Jewish traditions. These are contrary to Christ because they set up an authority alongside His Word.

- Baptism is not a mere symbol. When undergone with faith, it becomes a means of grace in God's hand and accords us a part in the death and resurrection of Christ.

- Jesus is God in all and every aspect of the term. When He took on humanity, He did not cease to be God.

LET'S PRAY

Almighty God, glorious in all You do,

our delight is in Your Son, our Savior,

in whom all the fullness of the godhead dwells bodily.

Seldom do we think of Him as we ought.

All too often we are taken up with our shibboleths

instead of making Him the focus of our lives and our endeavors.

Teach us to live with all the redeemed

in accordance with the gospel.

Make Christ so important to us

that our differences will fade in the light of His glory.

Cause us to seek from You and each other

nothing more than Jesus,

and be satisfied with Him

until the glorious day will come when,

by the power of grace,

we shall be like Him,

for we shall see Him as He is.

We plead in Jesus' name, amen.

QUESTIONS FOR DISCUSSION AND STUDY

1. On the basis of this passage, in what ways is the Old Testament Faith fulfilled in Christ?

2. Discus what was said in this section on baptism.

3. How and on what points does the experience of church life enlarge our views of the gospel, of Christ, and of the future redemption?

4. Discuss ways to develop an alert mind, guided and motivated by biblical truths.

5. Discuss the positives and negatives of tradition and the relation of tradition to the Word of God.

CHAPTER 5

Freedom in Christ

(COLOSSIANS 2:13–23)

13 And you, being dead in your intrusions and in the uncircumcision of your flesh, He co-enlivened with Him, forgiving us all the intrusions, 14 wiping out the handwriting against us consisting in statutes, which was contrary to us. He has taken it out of the way, nailing it to the cross. 15 Taking off the rulers and the authorities, He exposed them openly, triumphing over them while so doing.

16 Because of that, allow no one to judge you about eating and drinking, or with regard to a festival or a new moon or of Sabbaths 17 which things are a shadow of things coming, but the body is of the Christ. 18 Allow no one to deliver judgment against you in self-assumed humility and worship of the angels, things he has seen to no purpose by intruding into them, his pride being encouraged by his fleshly thinking, 19 and not holding on to the Head from whom all the body, by way of the joints and ligaments provided, and being connected, will grow together by God's doing.

20 If you died with Christ from the basic elements of the world, why, as though living in the world, are you subject to statutes: 21 "do not touch, nor taste nor handle," 22 which things are all meant to be destroyed by their use, according to the injunctions and teachings of men? 23 Which things truly have a reputation for wisdom

and self-imposed worship, of humility and of severe treatment of the body, but which have no honor in that they satisfy the flesh.

Up to this point, participation in the death and resurrection of Jesus had its primary reference to the Law, to ceremonies, and to what Paul described as the basic elements of the world. This is very much like what Paul had to say in Galatians 2:19-20: "Through [the dictates of] law I died to the Law, so that I might live to God. I have been crucified with Christ. It is no longer I who live, but Christ who lives in me. And the life I now live in the flesh I live by faith in the Son of God, who loved me and gave Himself for me" (see also Romans 7:1-5). Here the apostle refers to yet another death that was the Colossians' lot: death in sin (due to their participation in the sin and death of Adam). The resurrection of which Paul speaks next is to a new life by faith in the Son of God and by virtue of the new powers God has unleashed in the believer, so that he delights after God's law, longs to keep it, and is enabled to do so.

"And you." Paul reminds the Christians in Colossae that they were included in this wonderful reality. Their past could only be described as "being dead in your intrusions and in the uncircumcision of your flesh." The apostle's twofold description of their former situation is fascinating. The Greek term I have chosen to translate "intrusions" is commonly translated "trespasses," which is an excellent rendering of the word but for the fact it is so common that we have become inured to its meaning. Wanting to draw your attention to that meaning, I chose to startle you with a term you would not expect to find in this context.

Fundamentally, Paul was actually referring to trespassing, that is, to an unlawful intrusion into someone else's territory. This term (*paraptoma* in Greek) means exactly that. It is one of the many terms Scripture uses to designate the various aspects of sin. It means the arrogation of rights belonging to someone else, in this case to God. Every time we set ourselves up as the goal of our lives, every time we partake of forbidden fruit, every time we transgress a border God established, we are trespassing and will have to give account to God.

The Colossians had trespassed in the past by living for pleasure and by viewing their prowess as the sole source on which to rely for success. Now they were in danger of repeating the same mistake. They were trespassing by attributing to themselves and to rituals what only God in Christ can give.

The second term Paul uses to describe their former state is "in the uncircumcision of your flesh." This, of course, brings us back to what Paul said in 1:21 and 2:11–12. In the past, they were Gentiles, strangers, with no valid reference to Jewish ceremonies and, what is more important, with no reference to God. They were dead and bodily uncircumcised. They are not such any longer, and this they obtained, not by virtue of ritual, human effort, or enlightenment, but by the virtues of Christ.

Although trespassers and uncircumcised, we have been co-enlivened with Him; that is, with Jesus. He forgave us all the intrusions of the past, to which we ought not return by arrogating to ourselves the ability to obtain enlightenment or spirituality by way of ceremonies, ritual observances, and appeals to purportedly spiritual beings. In forgiving us, Paul says, God wiped "out the handwriting against us consisting in statutes, which was contrary to us." Paul is referring to the Law, to Jewish customs the Colossians were encouraged to embrace. The term *handwriting* refers to the ancient equivalent to a modern IOU—a written obligatory note.

Paul's words echo what Peter said in a similar context in Acts 15:10–11: "Why are you putting God to the test by placing a yoke on the neck of the disciples that neither our fathers nor we have been able to bear? But we believe that we will be saved through the grace of the Lord Jesus." Salvation is not just the forgiveness of sins. It is newness of life through participation in the resurrection of Christ.

In other words, to embrace such customs is to imply Jesus made no difference, or at least that He did not make enough of a difference, for if righteousness was achievable by law-keeping, "then Christ died for no purpose" (Galatians 2:21). In such a case, He is not all-sufficient, and we must now add to His achievements Hebrew roots, Messianic practice, the Passover Seder, circumcision, keeping a seventh-day Sabbath, Davidic dancing, a prayer shawl, the laying of phylacteries, a Second Blessing, and such.

"No," says Paul. Here is what God did with "the handwriting against us consisting in statutes, which was contrary to us. He has taken it out of the way, nailing it to the cross." The death of Jesus spells the removal of the law's demands on us as the grounds of salvation, of sanctification, of a spiritual life, or of anything else we may claim from God for ourselves. Jesus is all-sufficient, and we are to focus on him.

We skipped a discussing phrase to which we must now return: Paul says the Law was "contrary to us." Why describe God's wonderful law in such terms? Because we could not keep it. As a result, instead of being a means of salvation or sanctification, it became our accuser. Paul spelled this out, for example, in Romans 7:7-11:

> If it had not been for the Law, I would not have known sin. For I would not have known what it is to covet if the law had not said, "You shall not covet." But sin, seizing an opportunity through the commandment, produced in me all kinds of covetousness. For apart from law, sin lies dead. I was once alive apart from the Law, but when the commandment came, sin came alive and I died. The very commandment that promised life proved to be death to me. For sin, seizing an opportunity through the commandment deceived me and through it killed me (ESV).

So, as Paul put it to Peter in Galatians 2:16, "we know that a person is not justified by law-keeping."

Living under the domain of the Law meant the Colossians were under the domain of the rulers and the authorities, emanations that purportedly made up the Divine Fullness and called for an adherence to some or all of Jewish custom. But such a submission brought death, not life.

Paul describes these powers in terms that seem to be taken from the heretical terminology being taught in Colossae. The emanations were believed to control various levels of spiritual life and achievement. But they were all dealt with by Christ in his death and resurrection. Paul says that Jesus, "taking off" the rulers and the authorities, "exposed them openly, triumphing over them" in so doing. Jesus is Lord of all, above all, conqueror of all. What point is there, then, in turning from Him to serve lesser beings?

In an admittedly difficult passage Paul describes the emanations as if they clung to Christ, somehow trying to keep Him from the fullness of His accomplishments in the vain hope that, if they managed to hold on, a vestige of their powers would be preserved. But He "took them off." He "exposed them openly," much as Roman victors did when they returned from war and paraded their vanquished foes to the jeering, mocking, celebrating Roman crowd. The Roman Senate granted such a parade to the few whose victories were especially significant. They were called "triumphs." The general would ride into Rome with his booty and captives, "triumphing over them" to the jubilation of the crowd. Paul borrowed this lively picture to indicate the completeness of Christ's accomplishments. What room is left for rituals, ceremonies, or other human accretions? Jesus did it all. All to Him we give.

Such exactly is Paul's conclusion: because of that, "allow no one to judge you about eating and drinking, or with regard to a feast or a new moon or of Sabbaths." Food is a major issue in Scripture, greatly accentuated in Jewish tradition. But there is nothing in Scripture with regard to forbidden beverages. The rabbis enlarged on biblical injunctions and forbade a host of foods and food combinations. "You shall not boil a young goat in its mother's milk" (Exodus 23:19; 34:26; Deuteronomy 14:21) had become a prohibition disallowing all forms of cooking or consumption of milk and meat together (as if there were any danger of eating a chicken with its mother's milk), or even on the same plate.

The celebration of the New Moon is mentioned in the Law (Numbers 29:6), but had become an important feature of Second Temple Judaism, as was—and is—the careful observance of the calendric year. "Sabbaths" is in the plural because Paul is apparently not referring to the weekly Sabbath but to the various Sabbaths commanded in the Mosaic Law in relation to the feasts (Exodus 16:25; Leviticus 16:31; 23:32; 25:2). Please note: Paul's reference here is not to rabbinic custom but to the statutes of the Law as interpreted by the rabbis. No man was to hold the Colossians to account with regard to these statutes. No man has the right to oblige Christians by them. To the extent they were ever binding, they have found fulfillment in Christ. To the extent that the interpretations were wrong, they never had valid binding force.

Speaking of the Law, Paul goes on to describe the statutes of the Mosaic Law as "a shadow of things coming, but the body is of the Christ." Shadows are flat, dark contours of reality, void of detail, created by an object obstructing light. They are often distorted, depending on the angle of the light obstructed. The external, ceremonial aspects of the Law are to the Christ what a shadow is to an object: flat, no more than the dark contours of a wonderful reality, void of important detail.

Of course, there is in the Law real indication of the general contours of Christ, His work, and His message. "But the body is of the Christ." What are we to prefer, the shadow or the body? The Law or the Christ? Why, Paul is intimating, should one prefer the shadow to the reality when the shadow is but a partial representation of who Christ is, what He has done, how it affects us, and what He has taught? The shadow fades into insignificance in comparison with the reality. Jesus is a glorious Savior!

If such is true of the Law, given by God at Sinai, what ought to be said of rabbinic tradition? It is, of necessity, far less than the Law, less than a shadow of reality. It can offer less. Why, then, should we be taken up with such a tradition when the glorious reality of the Son of God is with us?

Paul therefore insists, "Allow no one to deliver judgment against you in self-assumed humility and worship of the angels." The Colossians were to resist every effort to bring them under the yoke of mystical experiences and Jewish ritual. They should not buy into the teaching that offers a means to communicate with angels or succumb to what Paul described as "self-assumed humility," which is nothing less than a show, one could almost say a parade (the contrast is striking: How does one parade or show off humility?) by submission to the rites and teachings of the heretics. These are things the purported teachers had seen in a trance, but they served no real purpose.

Paul is not arguing as to whether what the heretical teachers claimed to have seen was real or not. He assumes for the sake of argument it was. What good could such visions be? Can they contribute to a stable, mature kind of holiness, or do they create a sense of smug super spirituality? Do they encourage moral purity or pride? Do they truly bring one into God's presence or simply provide an emotional rush?

Paul answers: by "intruding into them," that is, into such trance-induced visions, one's pride is being encouraged by fleshly thinking. Rather than humility, pride is cultivated. Rather than spirituality, fleshly thinking becomes the order of the day because those undergoing such experiences cannot distinguish between the Spirit of God and their own spirits, between the presence of God and a sense of well-being. What is more, those who hold to such views are "not holding on to the head" who is Christ, the source of life, direction, and purpose for the body, "from whom all the body, by way of the joints and ligaments provided, and being connected, will grow together by God's doing."

Do you want to grow in Christ? Hold on to the Head rather than to every new-fangled idea that raises its head. Do you want to be more spiritual? Make sure you are connected to the body so that you benefit "by way of the joints and ligaments provided." Grow in the context God established for growth – the church. Don't separate. Don't seek the company of the initiates, of those who follow your patterns and embrace your pet doctrines and practices. It is by way of the joints and ligaments provided by God in Christ that the body will grow together, and "together" is the only way it will grow in a Christian way, "by God's doing" rather than through human effort.

That's the key. Spiritual growth is God's doing, not ours. It is a gift, not a reward. It is a fruit of divine blessing, not a product of human prowess. Fruit is cultivated, but all the cultivation in the world will not create a single fruit apart from the blessing of God.

It is time for Paul to draw some conclusions, which he does in 2:20–3:11. After that he will spell out some of the practicalities of what he said. The chapter division makes no sense. Dividing these verses from the first verses of chapter 3 is simply a mistake.

"If you died with Christ from the basic elements of the world." Paul is pointing to the implications of what was said in verses 8, 11–15 concerning those who have died and risen in Christ. Doctrine is not an intellectual pastime; it is meant to have measurable consequences. Paul is insisting that recognition of truths and an experience of them must lead to a certain way of life.

"If" here is in the indicative mood. It does not express doubt but a contingency of relationships. It might be better translated as "since." Later Paul would state, "You have died and your life is hidden with Christ in God" (3:3). He and the Christians in Colossae had died "from the basic elements of the world"; that is to say, "died away" from them. In modern parlance we would say "died a death which removed you from their control." The elements have no further sway over them, no claim to their obedience. Then "why, as though living in the world, are you subject to statutes?" Paul will soon inform us clearly as to the nature of the statutes to which he is referring, but what does he mean by "as though living in the world"? Where else were the Colossians living?

Look down for a moment to 3:1–3 (and see just reason out of many why the chapter division is so inappropriate). We'll explain that passage when we get to it, but we need to take in its surface meaning to understand what Paul is saying here. Yes, Colossae was in Asia Minor, and Asia Minor is definitely part of the world. But that is not where their real lives were, nor where the goal of their lives was to be found. They were in Christ. They were seated in heavenly places. Their lives were "hidden with Christ in God." They did not belong to the world and, in an ultimate sense, did not live here—they lived with Christ and in Him.

The false teachers promised their adherents they would be transported to the highest level of spirituality, freed from the world and its encumbrances. Well, "why, as though living in the world, are you subject to statutes ...?" Instead of a higher spirituality, they seemed to be busy with a lower level of spirituality than the gospel offers. That is exactly it: higher spirituality as the reward of human effort is always lower. No one can better what Christ can give.

Paul points to the kind of statutes with which the Colossians were taken up: "Do not touch, nor taste nor handle." He made no reference here to the moral aspects of the Law. Those abide and, as we can see from others of his writings, continue to play a role in the Christian life. We are never free to lie, covet, or steal. We must always love God, worship him according to His commandments, and love our fellow humans as we love ourselves. Those will be our eternal duties in heaven as they are on earth.

An unbiblical emphasis on ritual and external obedience always comes at the expense of moral duties. What we eat, drink, or touch is much easier to scrutinize than the spiritual and moral tenor of our lives. Misguided conceptions always tend to focus on the readily visible instead of the things that really matter.

It is characteristic of a kind of prideful fundamentalism, Jewish or otherwise, to be known primarily for its rejections and prohibitions: real Christians don't do this and don't do that; they avoid modern pop music and secular books, do not drink, do not dance, do not watch CBS or CNN, and do not cultivate friendships outside their own circle (unless they are involved in a form of evangelistic hypocrisy that purports to befriend people, but only to preach the gospel to them). True Christian holiness involves a kind of freedom that is taken up with moral purity in the fear of God and boldly enjoys the gifts God lavishes on us for our enjoyment, without making them a priority or becoming addicted to them.

The fact that our hearts have been inclined to live in such a way does not mean that the Law in its moral aspects is no longer binding. It means that our prayer has been answered: "Oh how I love your law! It is my meditation all the day... May my heart be blameless in your statutes ... in your steadfast love give me life, that I may keep the testimonies of your mouth" (Psalms 119: 97, 80, 88). As Paul put it in Romans 7:22, "I delight in the Law of God, in my inner being." Spirituality has to do with fulfilling "the righteous requirement of the Law," which is nothing less than "conducting ourselves in the Spirit" (Romans 8:4).

What is wrong with being taken up with issues such as dietary restrictions and prohibitions with regard to what we may handle? Simply this: it means we are taken up with material things, with the world from which we professedly seek escape, with things "all meant to be destroyed by their use." Instead of spirituality, what we have, in fact, is a gross form of materialism masquerading as a form of spirituality.

Further, the instructions to which the Colossians were inclined to submit were "according to the injunctions and teachings of men." Some of the prohibitions had their source in the Law as interpreted by the rabbis. Others were the product of human tradition. But, in Christ, even the ritual and ceremonial prohibitions imposed by the Law are no longer binding. To insist otherwise is nothing more than insisting on "the injunctions and teachings of men."

Having lost their validity as guides to a walk with God, the requirements of the Law had become merely human injunctions, the inventions and impositions of men to which rabbis added a plethora of rules, regulations, and instructions. As such, rather than being capable of leading those who observe them to a higher walk with God by according greater spiritual perceptions, they hold their adherents down and suppress the vitality of their spiritual walk. What is more, God is to be worshipped only as He commanded and not as men believe suitable. Hence, the observance of such rituals cannot be viewed as an act of obedience to God. It is, rather, submission to men.

Here Calvin is, again, insightful:

> It should be an axiom among all the godly, that the worship of God ought not to be measured according to our understanding; and that, consequently, the mere fact that it pleases us does not make a service lawful. It ought also to be an axiom that we owe God the humility of yielding obedience simply to His commands, so as *not to lean to our own understanding* (Proverbs 3:5).

The things, Paul says, that "truly have a reputation for wisdom and self-imposed worship, of humility and of severe treatment of the body" have "no honor" and only "satisfy the flesh." But their assumed reputation is one they do not deserve. They claimed observance of their rituals would lead to "wisdom" of a higher order, the knowledge of secrets only the initiates could obtain. Followers of these rules were noted for their "self-imposed worship," the kind of self-discipline often admired in the Greek and Roman cultures. They purported to be expressing "humility," admitting their need for enlightenment and additional spiritual help. They displayed a "severe treatment of the body" by refusing themselves the pleasures of eating, drinking, and touching others enjoyed so much.

But, Paul insists, they had no true honor because, rather than denying the flesh, they indulge it. Rather than being free from the world, they are focused on it. Rather than expressing devotion to God and to spirituality, they are engaged in a form of selfishness void of true spirituality.

Rather than encouraging humility, such practices encourage a prideful confidence in one's ability. They "satisfy the flesh."

LET'S SUMMARIZE

- In the past, the Colossian Christians were dead in sin to God and alive to the demands of law as the grounds of their relationship with God. In Christ, they share in His death and resurrection and are dead to sin and to law— any law. By His resurrection, they are alive to God.

- God in Christ must be the focus of our lives. Whenever we place something else at the forefront, we are intruding into property that belongs to God.

- In the past, the Colossian Christians were uncircumcised; that is to say, they had nothing to do with the covenants of grace. In Christ they were circumcised and shared in those covenants.

- The death of Jesus frees us from the demands of law as a basis for salvation or spirituality. Jesus is all-sufficient to provide as much and more. We are free from ritualistic obligations. These were but the shadow of Christ. He is the substance. Why leave the substance for the shadows?

- Ritualism and mysticism are not expressions of sincere humility but the means of arrogant pride. The way to true spirituality is a close connection with Jesus, the Head from which the body receives life.

- Extreme abstinence is not spirituality but a preoccupation with the things of the world, materialism masqueraded in the form of spirituality.

- Those who share in the death and resurrected life of Christ ought not to be taken up with earthly matters such as dietary laws and other rituals. Their lives are hid with Christ in God, and their hope is fixed on heaven, not on the earth.

- Christian spirituality expresses itself in holiness, not in elaborate rituals, mystical experiences, or esoteric knowledge.

LET'S PRAY

Great God of truth and righteousness,

who sees all things as they are,

not as we would have them appear to be,

we confess with sorrow and shame

that we find it easier

to focus on the tangible and the visible

than on Christ, on holiness, or on truth.

We tend to trust ourselves more than You.

We dare think it is within our power

to contribute to our walk with You.

As a result, we lose sight of Christ, the perfect Savior,

and deny the grace that saved and consecrated us.

Teach us to hunger truly,

to seek those things above,

where Christ sits at Your right hand,

and to conduct our lives in chastened holiness.

Forgive us our pride and cleanse us of it,

that You might have all the glory

through Jesus Christ, amen.

QUESTIONS FOR DISCUSSION AND STUDY

1. Discuss the way that ritual and professed esoteric knowledge encourage pride.

2. How does abstinence indulge the flesh?

3. What implications do you derive from what Paul had to say here about uncircumcision and circumcision?

4. Why and how does true spirituality lead to holiness?

CHAPTER 6

The New Man
(COLOSSIANS 3:1–11)

1 If, then, you were co-raised with the Christ, 2 seek things that are above, where the Christ is sitting at the right hand of God 3 because you died and your life has been hidden with the Christ in God. 4 Whenever the Christ, our life, is manifested, then also you with Him will be manifested in glory. 5 For that reason, kill your members on earth: fornication, impurity, passion, lust and covetousness (which is idolatry), 6 because of which God's anger is coming 7 and in which you conducted yourselves when you lived in these things. 8 But now put away you also all these things: fury, anger, malice, blasphemy, filthy speech from your mouth; 9 don't lie to one another, having removed the old man with his habits 10 and having put on the new man who is being renewed in full knowledge in compatibility with the image of Him who is creating him, 11 where there is no place for Greek and Jew, circumcision and uncircumcision, barbarian, Scythian, slave, freeman ... but Christ is everything (all) and in all.

Truth is meant to shape life. None of Paul's letters, indeed, none of Scripture is the product of an abstract intellectual exercise; what is written arose out of the real-life situations addressed. Paul was keenly aware of the fact that truth is the servant of duty, just as duty is the incarnation of truth, and that both truth and duty have to do with reality. For that reason, all of his letters include practical instructions and such instructions always follow a presentation of gospel truth. Paul now comes to the practical application of the principles he presented.

"If, then, you were co-raised with the Christ." Once again, the "if" here is indicative, not expressive of doubt but of contingency, of consequence. It is to be understood as "since." Paul speaks of the Colossian Christians as having died and risen in Christ. So far as he is concerned, none share in Christ's death without sharing in His resurrection, and none who share in His resurrection are free to live but in a manner consistent with that transforming reality. So he appeals to the Colossians: "Seek things that are above, where the Christ is sitting at the right hand of God."

You will recall that in 2:8-10, 20-22, Paul pointed out that, in contrast to their claims of a higher spirituality, the false teachers in Colossae were actually earth-bound materialists. That is what Paul is speaking of here. Of course, it is possible to see in this statement a call to spirituality in other areas as well, but Paul's immediate concern was with the false spirituality the Colossian heretics were promoting. He wants the Colossians to focus on Christ, on true spirituality, on heavenly things rather than on "touch not, taste not, and handle not" as the means to spirituality. Keeping kosher, observing the Seder, wearing a skull-cap, or any other form of ceremonial purity never made anyone holier.

Paul wants the Colossians to love God and keep His commandments. He wants them to avoid dependence on the legitimate pleasures of the world, to put God first in the order of their priorities. He wants them to have a broad, deep understanding of the power of the gospel by way of a broad, deep understanding of the glories of Christ's majesty and accomplishments. In short, he wants them to concentrate on what God did for them rather than on what they could do in an effort to scramble up the imaginary ladder of spiritual achievement.

"Because you died [past tense] and your life has been hidden [passive—God did it for them] with the Christ in God." Dying is about all a person can do in this regard, and even that did not come at his initiative. The death of which Paul speaks is not death in sin but death to law in the death of Christ.

Sin rendered mankind subject to law and its condemnation. That condemnation came about through law both by revealing their sinfulness and by pronouncing their judgment because of it. Mankind was then subjected to rules that forbade foods, drinks, and the touching of various objects. But the Colossian Christians had died with Christ and, in consequence, they died to law. They had also risen with Christ and the life they now lived, they lived by faith, apart from dependency on keeping the law for salvation or for holiness—except for the fact that the moral aspects of the Law continue to serve as a guide and a standard. The Colossians were not subject to the ceremonial aspects of the Law any more than Christ is subject to them.

Their lives were "hidden (and therefore secure) with the Christ (that is to say, the Messiah) in God." That was where their real life was to be found—not in the crass issues of life, but in the glorious realities of which they now enjoyed a foretaste and that were yet to come in fullness. What they have now is a guarantee and harbinger of what they were to be given: "Whenever the Christ, our life, is manifested, then also you with Him will be manifested in glory."

What they were to have is "glory." This is a repeated theme in Paul's letters and an important aspect of salvation as Paul would have us understand it. The apostle would make further reference to this glory in verses 4 and 10 of this chapter, and had already made reference to it in 1:27.

In his other letters we learn that glory, honor, immortality, and peace await those who seek to do good (Romans 2:7, 10), whereas sinning leads to a corruption of the divine image in man (Romans 3:23), in which man was created (1 Corinthians 11:7). Our hope is to be brought by grace to share again in the glory of that image (Romans 5:2; 8:21; 15:7; 1 Thessalonians 2:12; 2 Thessalonians 2:14; 2 Timothy 2:10), stupendous though it is (Romans 8:18; 2 Corinthians 4:17; 2 Timothy 4:8). For this purpose, the elect have been prepared (Romans 9:23). Sharing in His glory is to be realized in the coming of Christ (Colossians 3:4) and the resurrection (Romans 8:18–21, 29; 1 Corinthians 15:23). Our new nature is presently being formed in us by the Spirit (1 Corinthians 15:39; 2 Corinthians 3:18); that is how God has chosen to glorify His Son as Savior, Redeemer, and Christ (2 Thessalonians 1:10, 12; see also Romans 8:29).

It really is quite a thought; man was created in the image of God. That image was scarred and distorted by sin. It is to be renewed and enhanced in our salvation; we shall be glorified in and by Him, bear His image, and become a source of heavenly amazement. Beatified with His beauty, made holy with His holiness, clothed with His righteousness, and granted an eternal share in His majestic, happy perfections—with an important difference: our beauty is granted; His is inherent. Ours is contingent; His is eternal. Ours is by grace; His is by nature.

In light of these statements, we can better understand Paul when he says, "Whenever the Christ, our life, is manifested, then also you with Him will be manifested in glory." Glory is not to be had by any other means than by the Christ, who is our life. It is not to be had in its fullness at any other time but "whenever the Christ ... is manifested." It is not the reward of human endeavor, something man reaches out to obtain. Any who obtain glory "will be manifested in glory" (note the passive). It is not to be had except with Him and contingent on His being glorified.

The Christ of God is the essence of our life, because apart from Him we are lost in sin and in darkness, without God and without hope in the world. With Him we are alive toward God and, as a result, very much alive to life as it ought to be, to holiness, to spirituality, to God's law, and to the love of God. Because He lives, we too are alive, to overflowing.

The word *whenever* in relation to the manifestation of the Christ does not refer to multiple manifestations but to a single manifestation, the timing of which is unknown to man. The manifestation is the revelation of Jesus' fuller glory both as divine and as Christ. Second Thessalonians 1:10 speaks of the time "when he [that is, Christ] shall come to be glorified in his saints, and to be admired in all them that believe." The book of Revelation speaks of the time of Jesus' exaltation and glory in 1:12–17 and in chapters 5, 14:1–5; and 19:11–16.

In the past, the glory of Christ was hidden, at first within the developing folds of revelation prior to His coming and then in His humanity, culminating in His death and burial. It is now in the presence of God, unseen by human eyes. But the day of His manifestation will unquestionably come and, whenever that will be, then we who are in Christ, "with Him, will be manifested in glory."

His manifestation will be the occasion and the cause of our own. This is what Paul described in Romans 8:19–23 as "the revealing of the sons of God, the glory of the children of God," and "the redemption of our bodies." As he put it in 1 Corinthians 15:49–57:

> Just as we have borne the image of the man of dust, we shall also bear the image of the man of heaven. I tell you this, brothers: flesh and blood cannot inherit the kingdom of God, nor does the perishable inherit the imperishable.
>
> Behold! I tell you a mystery. We shall not all sleep, but we shall all be changed, in a moment, in the twinkling of an eye, at the last

trumpet. For the trumpet will sound, and the dead will be raised imperishable, and we shall be changed. For this perishable body must put on the imperishable, and this mortal body must put on immortality. When the perishable puts on the imperishable, and the mortal puts on immortality, then shall come to pass the saying that is written: Death is swallowed up in victory." "O death, where is your victory? O death, where is your sting?" The sting of death is sin, and the power of sin is the law. But thanks be to God, who gives us the victory through our Lord Jesus Christ.

"For that reason," — and what a good reason it is — "kill your members on earth." The members of which Paul speaks are habits of sin that have become so much part of us that they are like parts of our body, parts of who we are. *Kill* is a strong word, but hardly too strong for what we must do to our sinful habits. How are habits killed? By starvation. Instead of exercising and feeding them through submission to their persistent demands, we must refuse them.

What habits does Paul have in mind? Like all his lists, the one below is not meant to be exhaustive. It is a representative list of sinful habits common in Paul's day and that, to our shame and regret, are common today: "fornication, impurity, passion, lust and covetousness (which is idolatry), ... fury, anger, malice, blasphemy, filthy speech from your mouth; don't lie." We'll view them one by one.

The Greek word *pornea* is commonly translated "fornication." Fornication is the engagement in illicit sex of any kind. Licit sex is sex conducted between two of the opposite sex within the loving, giving framework of a covenantal relationship—a marriage. Any form of sex outside those confines is forbidden and comes under the category of fornication. It does not matter how much you love the other person, whether you are engaged or not, nor whether the relations are consensual. Sexual relationships must be maintained within the context of a biblical marriage. Paul would have his readers avoid all and any sexual relations outside those boundaries.

Much like today, Roman culture was extremely promiscuous, with homosexuality, bi-sexuality, bestiality, transsexuality, and unrestrained sexual activity widely accepted. Prostitution, both male and female, was legal. For Romans, who were used to the values implied by and the free practice of such activities, sex became something of an addiction. Breaking away from it was little less than a killing of a bodily organ. It involved a long, determined, self-denying refusal to satisfy desires that had become accustomed to immediate satisfaction.

Regardless of the cultural norms adopted by those among whom Christians live, God's Word is the standard by which we are to conduct ourselves. Its spiritual and moral goals should be ours at any cost.

The next word is *akarthsia*, generally translated "impurity," with reference to moral rather than ceremonial impurity. Such impurity is the engagement of one's mind with impure thoughts, be it through pornography or fantasizing (which is nothing but self-created pornography).

There is an important difference between sex and impurity. The Bible has nothing to say against sex as such. In fact, a whole book (the Song of Solomon) is devoted to the celebration of sexual love. The writer to the Hebrews stated without hesitation that marriage is to be "held in honor among all," and "the marriage bed is undefiled" (13:4). At the outset of history, God blessed Adam and Eve with the commandment to "be fruitful and multiply" (Genesis 1:28), and Scripture accords sexual relationships between husband and wife the honorable title of "knowing" one another (Genesis 4:1 and many others).

Scripture has nothing of the prudish attitude that characterizes many in matters of Exodus There is nothing wrong with a sexual scene in a book or a movie that is not intended to tantalize, arouse, or tempt, but simply and with the proper reservation serves to convey the reality being reported. There is nothing wrong with a husband or a wife desiring one another. Sexual impurity is another matter. Impurity refers to all forms of sexual engagement in the mind that does not serve a valid purpose but is meant to evoke sexual desire or satisfaction outside the context or marriage. True, a fine line is often all that separates the two. At times the line is in the mind and intent of the reader or the spectator, but—after all—holiness has to do with a walk before God in terms of mind and intent before anything else, and there it is very hard for us to deceive ourselves.

The next term is the Greek *pathos*, translated "passion." There is nothing wrong with passion. One should love God passionately. Husbands and wives should love one another and their children passionately. David expressed passion in his love for God, as did others before and after him. What Paul was speaking of here is hedonism, a culture that views the pursuit of pleasure as the meaning of life, a sensuality that is given over to bodily stimulations, be it by way of music, food, drink, drugs, sex, cruelty (sadism), or pain (masochism).

The Roman world was a world of pleasure in which human life had little value. Gladiators were taught to fight to the death. Roman feasts involved participants gorging themselves on servings of exotic meats and fruits prepared according to innovative recipes and presented in unusual, dramatic ways; inducing vomiting; and returning to eat in sumptuous surroundings, from costly tableware and with the accompaniment of music, the sound of waterfalls, and the patter-patter of male and female servers. Roman ceremony, political and religious, was designed to create the kind of pathos against which Paul warns his readers. Breaking away from such a culture is, likewise, little less than the killing of a bodily organ. It too involves a long, determined refusal to satisfy desires accustomed to immediate satisfaction.

The next Greek word is *epithumia*, which connotes desire, usually inordinate desire and therefore lust. Lust is most often an exaggerated desire for the satisfaction of a legitimate need. We need food and drink, human companionship, love, and respect. We need a house in which to live and clothes to wear. We need to know and understand, to be what God has made us and to realize the potential He has planted in each of us. There is nothing wrong with wanting such things. There is nothing wrong with ambition. But if we want them more than we desire to serve God, if we want more of them than we need, or are willing to sin in order to obtain them, we are guilty of lust. "Sheol and Abaddon are never satisfied, and never satisfied are the eyes of man" (Proverbs 27:20). "The leech has two daughters: Give and Give. Three things are never satisfied; four never say, 'Enough'" (Proverbs 30:15).

The Christian virtue of self-discipline is the opposite of the unrestrained, exaggerated and compulsive desire of which Paul spoke. Self-discipline is not easily achieved and is easily lost. Ask any active sports person how much effort it takes for her or him to develop and maintain the body tenor necessary for successful sportsmanship. Ask further how much effort is needed for the necessary abilities to deteriorate. Sin drives us to want more than we need, to hoard more than is reasonable. Self-discipline, an aspect of self-denial, requires careful, constant, consistent spiritual and moral exercise and the determined development of a spiritual and moral conscience by the study of God's Word and self-examination in light of what we have learned.

The next sin naturally follows desire: *covetousness*. Covetousness is the desire to have something that belongs to someone else: "You shall not covet your neighbor's house; you shall not covet your neighbor's wife, or his male servant, or his female servant, or his ox, or his donkey, or anything belonging to your neighbor" (Exodus 20:17). There is nothing wrong with wanting something, so long as what we want is legitimate and our desire is within spiritual and moral boundaries. It is wrong to want what belongs to others, all the more so if we want it because it belongs to someone else. You might want to have a new car or an available position at work because you need (or will simply enjoy) them, but be sure your motives are pure. Beware of jealousy. Beware of coveting.

Paul went on to describe covetousness as "idolatry." Why? What is the relationship between covetousness and idolatry? As we said, coveting involves wanting what others have. Its basic motive is wrong. It knows no boundaries and is inclined to set that desire above all other considerations. That is why Paul described it as idolatry. Only God must hold such a position in our hearts and lives. He demands the right to be first in our lives and commands us to conduct our lives in light of His legislated standards

"Because of which God's anger is coming." All of these sins are said to be reasons for the approaching anger of God.

God's anger is not a subject most preachers like to address. Nor is it one about which most people want to hear. But it is a truth we all need both to hear and proclaim. God hates sin and will not allow it to go unpunished. He is a holy God whose beautiful, holy righteousness stokes the very fires of hell "prepared for the devil and his angels" (Matthew 25:41) and will cast into it "the cowardly, the faithless, the detestable, as for murderers, the sexually immoral, sorcerers, idolaters, and all liars. Their portion will be in the lake burning with fire and sulfur, which is the second death" (Revelation 21:8). We cannot be true to the gospel without proclaiming this truth. Nor can we explain the cross except in light of God's terrible hatred of sin.

That anger "is coming." It is active, ever approaching. No event is indicated as standing between the present coming of God's anger and its arrival. By choosing the present continuous tense, Paul creates the kind of tension that puts his readers on their spiritual and moral toes. One can never tell when the process of coming will end, how near it is, and where it will catch us. Mankind would do well to live in light of that reality and mends its ways.

This is one of the ways the biblical message impacts our lives: by creating the very tensions we wish to avoid. We prefer to have everything nailed down so that there are no surprises. The Word of God is not fashioned to our likings but to our needs. We are called upon to live between the "not yet" and the "any moment now," indeed, often between the "already" ("these things happened to them as an example, but they were written down for our instruction, on whom the end of the ages has come" [1 Corinthians 10:11]) and the "not yet" ("see that you are not alarmed, for this must take place, but the end is not yet" [Matthew 24:6; see also 36–44]).

"[And] in which you conducted yourselves when you lived in these things." By reminding the Colossian Christians of their past, Paul is urging them not to return to their former ways by focusing on ritual and purportedly spiritual exercises instead of on the realities that serve to make up biblical holiness. Further, he calls upon them to exert still greater moral efforts: "But now put away you also all these things: fury, anger, malice, blasphemy, filthy speech from your mouth; don't lie to one another."

"Put away" is a conscious, deliberate act, here described as something that the Christians in Colossae were to do rather than wait until God did it for them. It involves intended moral action, an exercise of self-discipline that will lead eventually to the breaking of bad habits and the forming of new ones. It entails premeditation, self-examination, and the lack of moral compromise. Our goal is not to weaken the habits of sin but to rid ourselves of them. With that in mind, as Moule put it, we must not allow ourselves to "sin on a moderate scale."[12] Rather, we should work at killing sin every time it raises its ugly head, the very moment it does so. Such a putting away is never a once-and-for-all event. It is a constant process, a constant battle to be won when the Last Day comes and we are in the presence of God.

It is worth reminding ourselves that Paul addresses these warnings to Christians. Yes, Christians are susceptible to the worst of sin. They too—we too—need to be reminded that moral exertion in the fear of God is an ongoing duty. We are to put away, set aside, remove from ourselves and from the habits of our lives and to take control of those moments when we are so angry we do not control what we say or do. "Anger," not all of which will be unjustified, must never be allowed to be the sole determining factor of our actions.

There will be times when it will only be right to be angry. "God ... feels indignation every day" (Psalms 7:11) as He looks down on mankind's

---

[12] Moule, *Colossian and Philemon Studies*, 217.

wickedness. But "the anger of man does not produce the righteousness of God" (James 1:20). Certainly, anger should not be what characterizes us, or our relations.

Paul exhorts the Colossians to "put away ... malice." Regardless of what others do to us, we should never act toward them out of malice. We should not harbor any desire for their ill. The only way to do that is to avoid bitterness, and the only way to avoid bitterness is to forgive, heartily, sincerely. This we can do if we realize the worst done to us is but a tool in the hand of God. Unless He wills, no fire can so much as singe our clothes, no lion can harm us. However unkind people may be, we should turn the other cheek, go the extra mile, concede our cloak, and be slow to anger, quick to forgive, and brave enough to recognize that we can, by the grace of God, derive good out of every evil.

Blasphemy is the next sin the Christians are exhorted to put off. To blaspheme is to desecrate the honor of God by word or by deed, the avoidance of which is the logic behind the prohibition, "you shall not take the name of the LORD your God in vain, for the LORD will not leave him unpunished who takes his name in vain" (Exodus 20: 7). In the Roman era, as in our day, it was common to vow as well as to curse in the name of the gods. Christians are forbidden to do both ("Do not take an oath at all, either by heaven, for it is the throne of God, or by the earth, for it is his footstool, or by Jerusalem, for it is the city of the great King" [Matthew 5:34-35]).

We also blaspheme when we disparage the image of God in man by belittling someone in word or in deed, when we rob him or her of their dignity or of hope, and when we deny them the liberties and duties that are the privileges of mankind. Slavery is a form of blasphemy, as is prostitution, moral manipulation, deceit, scorn and the withholding of the basic necessities of life.

We blaspheme the name of God by lifestyles and actions that run contrary to our claim to love and serve God. It is not possible to honor God without honoring our fellow humans, nor can we truly love God unless we love our neighbor as ourselves. We should be very careful in all things that pertain to God, so as to honor Him at all times. We should be very careful of God's dignity. Loving Him inevitably means we are eager for others to love Him too, and that we exert ourselves in ways that honor Him rather than attach shame to His name. Israel failed in this respect by the way it conducted itself as a nation (Isaiah 48:11; Jeremiah 34:16; Ezekiel 20:9).

The next thing the Colossians were called upon to avoid is "filthy speech from your mouth. "Let no corrupting talk come out of your mouths, but only such as is good for building up, as fits the occasion, that it may give grace to those who hear" (Ephesians 4:29). I had become so accustomed to swearing that, upon my conversion, I discovered this was a habit not easily overcome. I cannot count the times I failed until I was finally granted success. The principle is simple: if what you want to say is not going to do good to the person who hears you, don't say it.

Finally, Paul calls upon the Colossians, "Don't lie to one another." This injunction comes almost exactly in the terms of Leviticus 19:11: "You shall not lie to one another." Honesty is a fundamental obligation. Lying is radically anti-Christian. Dishonesty destroys trust; it undermines the basis on which any healthy human relationship can be established. It is a kind of betrayal, a theft, a form of adultery, denying reality as it is and affirming a reality that does not exist. Those who fear God should be frankly and sacrificially committed to the truth.

God is the God of truth and truthfulness, of integrity. Our "yes" should be as solid as a rock; our "no" as unmovable as a mountain. Of necessity, this means that we will have to think a good deal more before we express ourselves, but I can assure you that this will be a welcome and helpful exercise. "When words are many, transgression is not lacking but whoever restrains his lips is prudent" (Proverbs 10:19). We would do well to heed the advice of Ecclesiastes; "Be not rash with your mouth, nor let your heart be hasty to utter a word before God, for God is in heaven and you are on earth. Therefore, let your words be few" (5:2).

Once again let us remember: this letter was addressed to Christians. It is people like us—you and me—who need to be reminded not to lie. This does not mean we should give expression to everything in our mind, or even that we should at all times relieve people of their false impressions. But it does mean we do not say an untruth. A Christian general may well have some of his forces feint in one direction in an effort to cause the enemy to concentrate his forces there, while he actually intends to focus an attack elsewhere. But lying is another matter.

In the past, the kinds of behavior proscribed by Paul were part of daily reality. But the Colossians had been converted. *Conversion* means change. When something is converted, it cannot remain the same. The Colossians are described as "having removed the old man with his habits and having put on the new man who is being renewed in full knowledge in compatibility with the image of him who is creating him." The change they had undergone involved removing the old man, whom they were in Adam, "with his habits" of sin. Christians are no longer subject to the control of sin, although often and in many ways are still exposed to its enticements.

The Colossians had then "put on the new man." They had clothed themselves with whom they were in Christ. The sinful habits developed before their conversion no longer had a valid hold over them, but the practical force of those habits needed to be broken and replaced. Having put off, they put on and were to continue to do so by the inculcation of biblical principles and biblical motives, and by the insistent development of habits of holiness.

They were not alone in the struggle against the habits of sin and its demands. The new man that they were in Christ "[was] being renewed" by the ongoing activity of God the Spirit; they were being granted" full knowledge" in the sense of a personal, intimate understanding and embracing of God and His will through which they were being increasingly changed "in compatibility with the image of Him who [was] creating him." The image into which they were being changed was the image of God. The "him" being created was the new man. The one creating was God Himself. God's marvelous work of salvation began with faith and repentance, but there was a lot more to it than that. He was at work in their hearts by His Spirit, transforming men and women, boys and girls, Jews and Gentiles, slaves and freemen into His own image.

The ravages of sin were being removed. Increasingly, the beauty of God's glory was shining forth in them. He was strengthening them in their conflict, rebuking and encouraging them when they failed, renewing their desire for His ways, comforting them, and ever motivating them to greater holiness, sincerer humility, broader kindness, and more substantial integrity. God's people were being prepared for life in heaven in the happy, holy presence of God.

This is the moment to draw your attention to an important fact: the "you" from verse 5 onward is plural. Paul is not addressing individuals in the church but the body as a whole. It is much easier to break bad habits and replace them with good ones when we enjoy the support and encouragement of community. It is much easier to break away from one's former way of life and adopt another when we are in loving, exhorting, rebuking, inspiring, motivating fellowship with others engaged in the same spiritual and moral pilgrimage. That is one of the reasons why church life is so necessary to Christians. If you have noticed the similarity between the Spirit's work and that of the church, do not be surprised. The Holy Spirit uses the church for the accomplishment of His purposes. The church is God's habitation through the Spirit (Ephesians 2:22).

As a community the Colossians had put on Christ. As a community they had clothed themselves with the new man. As a community they were being remade into the image of the Creator. No individual can by himself reflect the fullness of the infinite glory of God. All of redeemed humanity cannot do that, let alone any individual. John heard no solos sung in heaven, no individual performances. What he saw was a congregation so large it could not be numbered.

The more united in Christ the church is, the more effectively it can reflect the image of Christ and the more effectively it can serve for the formation of that glorious image in each individual Christian. We need one another to serve God in Christ as we ought. The new man is you and me, the pastor and the elder, the deacon and the evangelist, the old and the young, the wise and the foolish, the strong and the weak, together in Christ.

In this new man former distinctions have no place. Their foundations have been removed by the death and resurrection of Christ. "There is no place for Greek and Jew, circumcision and uncircumcision, barbarian, Scythian, slave freeman ... but Christ is everything (all) and in all." That's it. That's the point Paul had been making. Christ is everything. He is all and in all.

If you have Him, you need no more. There is no advantage to being a Jew and none in becoming or acting like one. If you lack Him, you have nothing, regardless of whatever pretensions may be attached to what you have. Nothing else matters. No demiurge, no tradition however sanctified by years and adorned by rabbis, no angel, no abstinence, and no indulgence could ever match Him, let alone add to His completed achievements. Jesus did it all. Jesus is doing it all by His Spirit. The Colossians were no longer viewed as "Greek and Jew, circumcision and uncircumcision, barbarian, Scythian, slave and freeman." They had been circumcised. They had been freed. They had been elevated. They had been united with Christ and, in Him, were equal one to another. If they focused on Christ, they would have in Him all they needed in an abundance that passed comprehension and exceeded every holy aspiration.

LET'S SUMMARIZE

- Christian Truth is meant to shape our conduct. The more we understand truth, the better equipped we are to be what God would have us be.

- The future is with us in a meaningful way, in the present.

- In the future we will have glory: the restored image of God in which mankind was originally created.

- Christ is the essence of our life, hope, longing, and confident expectation. We are to kill the habits of sin that have become like members of our bodies.

- We must break away from a culture of pleasure seeking and discipline ourselves to seek holiness.

- God hates sin and will punish it; the punishment is already on its way and could fully appear any moment, so we must live carefully.

- We must live while maintaining the tension between what is and what will be, between fulfillment and expectation.

- We are being transformed as a community in Christ and should demonstrate this process by how we treat one another. There should be no abuse, no selfishness, no cruelty, no distinctions, and no taking advantage of weakness; we must conduct our congregational life focused on Christ and not on ourselves.

LET'S PRAY

God of our lives and of our salvation,

our lives are hidden with Christ in You,

and our glory is hidden with Him.

One in Christ in spite of our differences,

different yet one,

we are to live without dissensions and without suppressions, in love and holy, happy harmony.

We thrill at the thought of our calling

and cringe at the thought of our weaknesses and failings.

Help us, Lord.

Continue your work of transformation.

Teach us the self-discipline that is so necessary for holiness

and contributes to happiness in You.

Glorify Yourself in us,

and we will give You praise

through Jesus Christ our Lord, amen.

QUESTIONS FOR DISCUSSION AND STUDY

1. Discuss the value of theology.

2. What do you consider to be the main point of this passage?

3. Look back on your study of glory. Is there anything you need to amend, add, or subtract from your conclusions?

4. Review the specific sins Paul mentioned in this passage. How are they relevent to church life? What do you need to correct in your conduct in church?

Chapter 7

The Perfect Bond
(Colossians 3:12–17)

12 So as God's holy chosen ones, and having been loved, put on great sympathy, kindness, humility, meekness, patience, 13 bearing one another and forgiving each other. If anyone has a complaint against anyone—just as the Lord forgave you, you forgive as well. 14 Above all of these, love, which is the bond of perfection. 15 And let the peace of the Christ rule in your hearts, to which you (plural) were actually called in one body, and be thankful. 16 Let the Word of the Christ indwell among you richly, teaching and admonishing yourselves with psalms, hymns and spiritual songs, with grace in your hearts singing to God, 17 and everything whatsoever you (plural) do, speaking or acting, do everything in the name of the Lord Jesus, giving thanks to God the Father through Him.

What follows is also in the plural. Taking note of this little fact will help us get the point of Paul's message.

"There is no place for Greek and Jew, circumcision and uncircumcision, barbarian, Scythian, slave freeman ... but Christ is everything (all) and in all, so as God's holy chosen ones, and having been loved, put on great sympathy, kindness, humility, meekness, patience, bearing one another and forgiving each other. If anyone has a complaint against anyone ..." Paul is spelling out the practical implications of the demands that grace put upon the Colossians. They were God's holy chosen ones and were required to act as such. They were holy because God had made them holy by the sacrifice of His Son and the workings of His Spirit; He had cleansed them of sin, released them from its compelling bondage, put His law in their hearts, and made them His in a special way. They were holy because God chose and separated them from the mass of sinful humanity to be holy and without blame before Him. In spite of their many sins, they were God's chosen ones. They did not choose Him; He chose them. They loved because He first loved them, "and having been loved," it was their duty to love their fellow Christians by putting on the characteristics of true love, all of which are necessary to love as one body in Christ:

First, "great sympathy." The apostle is speaking of the ability and the honest willingness to see things from the other person's point of view, with his interests as close to one's heart as one's own. He is speaking of the ability to share another's sorrows, understand his concerns in a loving manner, and support him as he fails; of doing for others what you would want them to do for you. This kind of sympathy is the opposite of selfishness; it is a reflection of the beauty of Christ, who bore our pains and sorrows and underwent the temptations and trials of life we experience, and is therefore able to succor us to the full extent of our need and beyond. His sympathy toward us should be the grounds and motivation of ours toward others.

Such sympathy is especially necessary for Christians of diverse backgrounds and social standings because it enables them to live together in gospel harmony, sharing the grace of God and rejoicing in his goodness. An openness to other cultures, a willingness to bear with radically different personalities, and a realization that our way of understanding or doing things might not be the only way are necessary for a happy marriage, an edifying church life, and a stable society.

"Kindness" is grace's next requirement. Kindness is a good-natured willingness to please others and do them well. Its relation to sympathy is obvious. In his letter to the Philippians, Paul called upon his readers, "If there is any encouragement in Christ, any comfort from love, any participation in the Spirit, any affection and sympathy, complete my joy by being of the same mind, having the same love, being in full accord and of one mind. Do nothing from selfish ambition or conceit, but in humility count others more significant than yourselves. Let each of you look not only to his own interests but also to the interests of others." He then set before them the supreme example of kindness: "Have among yourselves this mind-set, which was in Christ Jesus, who though He was in the form of God did not count equality with God a thing to be grasped, but emptied Himself, by taking the form of a servant, being born in the likeness of men. Being found in human form, He humbled Himself by becoming obedient to the point of death, even death on a cross" (2:1–8). Christ's kindness and His humble generosity should be the grounds and motivation of ours toward others.

Church life is one of the important contexts in which we have both opportunity and need for kindness. It is where we give ourselves to others for God's sake as disciples of Jesus. Like in a family and, to a slightly lesser degree, in society, a sincere concern for others is what oils the hinges of relationships and transforms them into positive experiences of the kind of grace that is God-like because it exemplifies the gospel.

Kindness leads us to be alert, aware of, and sensitive to others and their needs. It means that we hold the door for the person entering the building behind us, that we give others leeway and forgive them liberally when they err. Kindness means that we are sincerely and practically committed to other people's welfare and do not act as if the world revolves around us. Kindness makes us patient under trial and generous when in need. Kindness is simply Christlikeness.

The next spiritually moral characteristic to which Paul calls the Colossians is "humility." Once again, the relationship between humility and the former qualities is obvious. Sympathy and kindness are the products of humility because humility is what teaches people to love their fellow humans as they love themselves; humility forbids an individual from thinking his concerns, joys, needs, fears, wants, and ambitions have the right to highest priority.

Humility reminds us that others are worth as much and dear to God as much as we consider ourselves to be. Humility is what enables husbands to love their wives, wives to accept their husbands' leadership, parents to lovingly respect their children as they bring them up in the Lord, and children to follow their parents' lead by obeying their well-intentioned demands. It is also what enables Christians to bear one another's burdens, forgive each other and live together in harmony in spite of their differences.

Pride, on the other hand, is one of the most destructive forces on the face of the earth. It has brought more suffering to mankind than anything else. It lay at the root of Nazi arrogance and of all historical imperialistic aspirations. It laid the ground for Western colonial abuse of Africa, for the suppression of nations under the heel of Islam and of so-called Christianity, for the heinous slave trade, and for both the First and Second World Wars. Pride destroys families, divides churches, and paves a straight path to hell.

We need to remind ourselves how Christ humbled Himself, became one of us, underwent our temptations, experienced our misunderstandings, misrepresentations, and mocking rejections, bore our sins in His own body on the tree, suffered, died, and was buried. His humility for our sakes should be the grounds and motivation of ours.

Next, Paul calls the Colossians to "meekness." In Roman times, meekness was considered a fault, not a virtue. Prowess was either military or political, and the two were often intertwined. Morality, a humble fear of God and unselfish liberality were signs of feebleness of mind or heart—or both. Today's values hardly differ. We have merely added keeping up with the Joneses, being aggressive salesmen or entrepreneurs, and standing up for ourselves in society. Paul called the Colossians to go against the grain of their society's values, as we are called to go against ours, and be known for meekness.

Meekness is not evidence of weakness; it takes a large degree of emotional security to agree to appear to be weak. Nor is meekness an expression of an inability to cope with reality or a lack of ambition or drive. Meek individuals can be ambitious and highly motivated, as was Jesus. A meek person is gentle, not self-assertive, although he may very well be capable of projecting a sense of rectitude and authority that will move others to acknowledge his authority.

Living together as we ought, in the family, at church, or in society, involves a good deal of compromise. Even when we think we're right, we often need to compromise until others come (if they come) to see things as we do. While it is wrong to comprise fundamental principles, we should not make everything a matter of conscience. It is right and good to be highly principled, but meekness should be part and parcel of our principles.

We should beware of being over-righteous (Eccl. 7:16). The Pharisees were over-righteous when they forbade healing the sick on the Sabbath or the plucking of grains to satisfy hunger. Paul warned the Roman Christians not to impose their sensitivities on those who did not share them (Romans 14:1–12). We must respect each other's liberties at the same time that we respect their sense of duty. Living together in the family, a church, or in society requires a meekness that does not seek to impose one person's personality or preferences on another but makes room for frank, respectful, gracious discussion, resulting either in continued disagreement or laying the grounds for shared understanding.

Our Lord exemplified a dignified, conquering meekness that should serve as a beacon and a call for us. His meekness as He lived on earth and related to people like us should be the grounds and motivation of ours as we relate to God and to others.

Patience is obviously related to meekness. Meekness leads to patience, which in this case is described by Paul as "bearing one another and forgiving each other. If anyone has a complaint against anyone." Paul was not discussing Christian character in the abstract; he was addressing a situation in which a distortion of the Christian Faith was introduced as a means of higher spirituality and which, in fact, served to create a lower state of contention, competition, pride, insensitivity to one's own failings, and blindness to the qualities of others. In such a context, differences between people are accentuated and harmony is unlikely.

Patience inevitably means "bearing one another," and the willingness to do so is necessary in any human context because none of us is perfect. "We all stumble in many ways" (James 3:2).

Consider a man and wife "bearing one another" in marriage. Angels neither wed nor are given in marriage. We marry precisely because we're not angels (If only we remembered that, we'd be spared many a disappointment!). Marriage is a challenging, edifying, sanctifying, humbling experience in which we can learn the validity of much of what Paul has to say in this portion of God's word. As much can be said of church life and of life in society.

Bearing one another means forgiving each other if anyone has a complaint against anyone. One would wish the *if* here expressed doubt. It does not. Human reality makes it clear: we often offend one another and, at least as often, have complaints one against another. *If* here is the now-familiar if of contingency meaning, "when" or, if you wish, "since you will undoubtedly have complaints the one against the other."

Because there is not a human relationship in which any one of the partners never has a complaint against another, this injunction is extremely valuable. A forgiving attitude is necessary to those who have been forgiven. Remember our Lord's warning:

> The kingdom of heaven may be compared to a king who wished to settle accounts with his servants. When he began to settle, one

was brought to him who owed him ten thousand talents. And since he could not pay, his master ordered him to be sold, with his wife and children and all that he had, and payment to be made. So the servant fell on his knees, imploring him, "Have patience with me, and I will pay you everything." And out of pity for him, the master of that servant released him and forgave him the debt.

But when that same servant went out, he found one of his fellow servants who owed him a hundred denarii, and seizing him, he began to choke him, saying, "Pay what you owe." So his fellow servant fell down and pleaded with him, "Have patience with me, and I will pay you." He refused and went and put him in prison until he should pay the debt. When his fellow servants saw what had taken place, they were greatly distressed, and they went and reported to their master all that had taken place.

Then his master summoned him and said to him, "You wicked servant! I forgave you all that debt because you pleaded with me. And should not you have had mercy on your fellow servant, as I had mercy on you?" And in anger his master delivered him to the jailers, until he should pay all his debt. So also my heavenly Father will do to every one of you, if you do not forgive your brother from your heart (Matthew 18:23–35).

How should forgiveness be granted? Paul does not leave us with the question; he said, "Just as the Lord forgave you, you forgive as well." The gospel teaches us to treat one another as God has treated us. He sought us when we did not seek Him. He prepared the grounds for our forgiveness although He had a well-established grievance against us. He wooed us with His kindness, without sacrificing His justice. He firmly but lovingly brought us to the bar of His justice and showed us our guilt, and then He moved us by his tender, mighty mercies and the gracious promises of the gospel to turn to him and be forgiven. When we repented, He laid no further demands on us but that we love Him sincerely. Since then we failed repeatedly, but He continues to forgive with a liberality that transcends imagination. "Just as the Lord forgave you, you forgive as well."

The apostle proceeds to tell the Colossians what they should put on: "Above all of these, love." Of course, love is expressed in all the aforementioned characteristics: sympathy, kindness, humility, meekness, patience, bearing one another, and forgiving each other. It is the motive behind them all. But why should a slave love his master, and what kind of transformation must the master undergo to love his slave? Why should a Jew love a Gentile or a Gentile a Jew? The answer is ready: because of the gospel, which recognizes no such distinctions and calls people from every nation under the sun to love and worship God, and to do so, among other ways, by loving one another. How could they love each other when they differed from one another and had such a history of mutual exclusion? Once again, the answer is ready: by the grace of God, by the power of the gospel, by the moving of the Spirit.

Love, then, is "the bond of perfection," or perhaps better, the perfect bond. Nothing binds better than love. Nothing binds us firmer to God than His love for us. Nothing blinds us more to other people's faults, moves us to care for them, bear with them, and sacrifice for them more than love. It is the perfect bond, capable of uniting diverse individuals who would not normally relate to one another by demanding of them, exemplifying to them, and motivating them toward a love that captures the heart and drives them to admit most willingly: "we love because He loved us first" (1 John 4:19).

Rather than engaging in conflict, competition, or the tendency to compare themselves with others, Paul calls upon the Colossians, "Let the peace of the Christ rule in your hearts." Be at peace with one another by virtue of the gospel. Be at peace with one another as Christ has made peace between you and the Father.

Could there be a greater difference than the divide between Him and us? He is holy and we are unclean. He is wise beyond measure and we are foolish beyond anything we can imagine. He is good and we are selfish. He is righteous and we are quick to take advantage of others' weaknesses. He is eternal and we depend on Him, on food, drink, air, and sleep. We rebelled against Him, corrupted His Word and abused His world, worshipped the creature rather than the Creator, and preferred temporal pleasure to eternal holiness. Yet He loved us with an everlasting love and, at the price of His Son, established peace between us.

That peace should "rule" in our hearts, so that we are unruffled by those who differ from us and never feel threatened by another's opinion or a contrary custom. Bedouin custom requires one to belch at the end of a meal to show satisfaction. Try that at a dark-suit dinner party in, say, France or England. Who is to say one custom is better than another? Middle Easterners embrace and kiss; why is that any less acceptable than a handshake? Blacks will often sway as they worship, while "cultured" whites stare frozen at the preacher. Which is more appropriate? There should be peace among us. The peace Christ established between the Father and us should rule our hearts. It should govern our reactions to those who differ from us.

"To the which peace you were actually called in one body." There is a reason, the apostle insists, that we were actually called in one body. After all, God could have chosen to create two—or more—bodies of Christ. He could have established a Gentile church and a Jewish church. He could have established a church for freemen and one for slaves, one for women and one for men, one for Spanish speakers and one for those who know English (or, for that matter Greek, Korean, or Hebrew), one for blacks and for whites. Oh yes, and one for Presbyterians and one for Baptists, one for Arminians and one for Calvinists. But He didn't. He established one church for all. Existing divisions are man-made. They run contrary to God's purposes, contrary to the gospel, and contrary to the essential nature of the church.

The church is to be one. The church is a fellowship of grace to which anyone can belong on the grounds of grace in Christ and only on those grounds. There is no room for the compartmentalization of the church. There is no biblical basis for the divisions that exist in the church. The church is to include Gentiles and Jews; freemen and slaves; women and men; Spanish, English, Greek, and Hebrew speakers; blacks and whites; Baptists, Presbyterians, Calvinists, and Arminians. These are to mesh and clash and be sanctified and grow together as they worship God and serve Him as one body. They are to learn from and love one another sincerely in spite of their differences and the difficulties these differences create. God's intention is to "gather all up into one." (John 11:52). His "plan for the fullness of time is to unite all things in him, things in heaven and things on earth" (Ephesians 1:10). He is doing that through the gospel. That is what we should be doing.

Christians acknowledge this truth. We pay it frequent lip service, and sometimes we even reach over the fences that our lazy preferences for comfort and sinful pride have created. We then consider ourselves exemplary, large-hearted, and exceptionally kind. The truth is, we betray the gospel by allowing the fences to exist in the first place. We should not reach over them; we should break them down. Like President Reagan in Germany when the wall still divided Berlin, we should "tear down this wall!"

We are called into one body to exemplify a peace that transcends differences and gives expression to God's ultimate eschatological goal: to undo the consequences of sin; to create a united, redeemed humanity, the members of which live together on the grounds of God's grace and enjoy a God-centered harmony that gives Him glory; to restore Eden at the expense of conflict.

Is Christ not sufficient to unite us? Are we to allow culture, language, race, social strata, or doctrinal differences that do not touch upon the essence of the Faith to divide what God has united in Christ? Is our culture or language or comfort more important than the Savior? The church is to be a harbinger of what is to come, a demonstration of the power of God and of the grace of the gospel. The church is to be a visible enactment of the future, when the wolf and the lamb will lie together and the ox and the bear will feed beside each other. What are we saying by our divisions? What message are we conveying to the world?

Our next mission is indicated by Paul's injunction: "And be thankful." Let's put that in context: "As God's holy chosen ones, and having been loved, put on great sympathy, kindness, humility, meekness, patience, bearing one another and forgiving each other. If anyone has a complaint against anyone—just as the Lord forgave you, you forgive as well. Above all of these, love, which is the bond of perfection. And let the peace of the Christ rule in your hearts, to the which you were actually called in one body, and be thankful."

Thankful for what? Thankful for being "called in one body." Thankful for the privilege of belonging to the church of Christ. Thankful for the fact that grace is the grounds for our membership. We do not need to learn another language, adopt another culture, improve or reduce our social standing, or subscribe to a denominational confession. Nor must we embrace the Colossian error, worship angels, or adopt Jewish custom. All who are in Christ are "called in one body." If we trust in God through Christ for salvation, if we acknowledge His glory and seek to love and serve Him, we belong to Christ and are therefore members of His one body. Nothing more is required.

"As they went along the road they came to some water; and the eunuch said, "Look! Water! What prevents me from being baptized?" [And Philip said, "If you believe with all your heart, you may." And he answered and said, "I believe that Jesus Christ is the Son of

God."] And he ordered the chariot to stop; and they both went
down into the water, Philip as well as the eunuch, and he baptized
him (Acts 8:36–38 NASB).

If then God gave the same gift to them as he gave to us when we
believed in the Lord Jesus Christ, who was I that I could stand in
God's way?" When they heard these things they fell silent. And
they glorified God, saying, "Then to the Gentiles also God has
granted repentance that leads to life" (Acts 11:17–18).

Next, Paul says to the Colossians, "Let the Word of the Christ indwell
among you richly."

The phrase is unusual. It appears only here. "The Word of Christ" is
nothing other than the Word of God, the Word of the gospel. Christ only
spoke what the Father gave Him to say. His message is to indwell the fellowship of the saints. It is to be their major characteristic, the focus of their
church life, the guide and arbiter of all differences. It is to indwell them by
the reading, teaching, and contemplating of God's Word (a clear indication
of the importance of preaching in the life of a congregation). The Word of
Christ points to His sufficiency and pulls us back every time we deviate.
We need the Word of Christ to conduct our church life as it ought to be
conducted. We do not need the word of tradition or of ecstasies who claim
additional revelation. As we focus on Christ, we focus on His Word.

Next, as the Word of Christ indwells among Christians, they are to
be engaged in "teaching and admonishing yourselves with psalms, hymns
and spiritual songs." Here is a solid standard for song in the church. There
is little, if any, distinction between psalms, hymns, and spiritual songs in
Scripture, and commentators differ greatly as to the distinctions they
draw, perhaps evidence of the lack of a solid basis for their arguments.
One or another of the terms might indicate singing with the accompaniment of music and another without, but the minute distinctions that may
exist are really unimportant. According to Paul, singing has an important
role in the life of the church. It has to do with teaching and admonishing.

The main purpose of song in the church is not self-expression but
instruction and admonition (an archaic word for "rebuke" or "call to
duty"). What we sing should, therefore, have substantial content. The
music should serve the words; it should never blanket them. If we sing
without thought, or if we hear a song and cannot decipher the words,
there is something fundamentally wrong. If the words are tacked on as a

justification for the music, or if we sense that the words are forced onto the music rather than the music serving to express and emphasize the words, the song is sub-Christian. Emphasis should be on the words, not on the music, and certainly not on the musicians.

While there is room for emotion in the church (woe betide a church in which there is no emotion), there is no room for emotionalism; our singing should be full of biblical content. It should do more than say "Hallelujah" or "I love you, Jesus," or even "You're holy." It should focus on the biblical message and its application to our lives. It should speak of the glory of God, His majesty, being, and attributes; of creation and the fall; of law and grace; of the incarnation; of Christ's life and teaching, His crucifixion, death, resurrection, and ascension; of redemption; of conflict with sin; of hope, victory, and the glory of God.

Yes, Christian hymnody should be theology put to music. Hymns, psalms, and spiritual songs should teach. They should inform us of our faith, call us to our duties, rebuke us for our failures, remind us of our comfort, and express our longing, determination, and hope in Christ to be all God would have us be.

Next we are told how we should sing: "with grace in your hearts singing to God." First, we should sing with grace in our hearts; that is to say, out of the experience of the gospel. Our singing should be an outburst of understanding of what God did for us through the gospel. Having been taught and admonished, and having come to a fresh or a refreshed comprehension of the wonderful grace of God, we sing, and we sing what we have been taught. We simply have to sing! We have to vent our renewed, thrilled appreciation of God and His kindness toward us in Christ Jesus. We have to respond in repentance, gratitude, hope, and commitment.

Second, and this is part of the point of Paul's letter to the Colossians as a whole, the "we" who should sing should be the community. Paul is not vying against individual worship, nor was he forbidding solos any more than he was forbidding an individual leading in prayer. He is concerned because the Colossian Christians were being encouraged by the false teachers to aspire to something beyond the normal experience of Christians. They were being told they should set themselves apart by adding to what they (and others) had received in Christ. But as we have seen, Paul insists there is nothing beyond Jesus. There is nothing beyond what the Savior has achieved.

We've also seen Paul insist on the unity of the church. He would now have that unity expressed in song—there should be more "we" in our singing than "I." We should sing as a community of the redeemed, conscious of the fact that we are not redeemed on our own, nor do we worship on our own. Our worship in song (and song is not the only way we worship when we come to church) should be a foretaste of what is yet to be for all eternity: "Then I heard what seemed to be the voice of a great multitude, like the roar of many waters and like the sound of mighty peals of thunder, crying out, 'Hallelujah! For the Lord our God the Almighty reigns'" (Revelation 19:6).

Third, our singing should primarily be directed "to God." On the one hand, we teach and admonish one another in song. On the other, we worship. But we never entertain. We speak one to another (which leaves room for solos and for a choir) and to God. But we do not perform, and there is no room for clapping in appreciation of the choir any more than there is room for us to clap in response to a sermon or an expression of holiness.

Finally, Paul calls upon the Colossians to focus on Christ as they aspire after increased spirituality: "And everything whatsoever you do, speaking or acting, do everything in the name of the Lord Jesus, giving thanks to God the Father through Him." The immediate application of such an admonition is related to the Colossians' spiritual endeavors, but there is no sphere in life in which we are free from serving God or seeking to grow in grace and in the knowledge of His ways.

"Everything," Paul says, "whatsoever," without distinction; whether it is washing dishes or driving your car, teaching a Bible lesson or relating to your spouse, singing a hymn or disciplining your children, at work or at play or in your spiritual life, in "speaking or acting, do everything in the name of the Lord Jesus." Don't aspire to go beyond Him. Relate all you do to Him, and whatever you cannot do in the name of the Lord Jesus, don't do. That is spirituality. That is the height to which you should aspire: "everything in the name of the Lord Jesus," with one important addition that will bring us back in a full circle to Christ: "giving thanks to God the Father through Him."

In other words, do everything as an act of worship and as an expression of gratitude to God for Him.

Let's Summarize

- God's love for us apart from any worthiness on our part must motivate us to love others in the same way. To that end He called and consecrated us.

- Understanding this we must undertake humility, patience, and forgiveness—all necessary for church life as well as for family and social life.

- Love is the perfect bond because it takes on Christ-like characteristics: giving rather than seeking to receive and ignoring failures, weaknesses, and distinctions.

- Live in peace with one another in church (and the family and society). That is our calling because it is God's ultimate intention to unite all in Christ.

- Focus on Christ, not on ceremony, ritual, angels, or knowledge.

- Sing heartily with understanding. Have grace in your hearts.

- Do all for God in Christ and do not be self-serving as were the Colossian heretics.

Let's Pray

The only wise God, who made the world

and has purposed its redemption through Christ,

who will bring all things into subjection to Christ

and unite all things in Him,

we adore You for Your wonderful plan.

We thrill at the thought

that the awful effects of sin will be undone

and that all the world will be made subject to Christ.

Help us subject ourselves to Him now most willingly.

Help us live with others by focusing on Your Holy Son,

by ignoring what sin would use to divide

and by relating to others selflessly

rather than seeking to compete.

Give us grace to show grace,

and by this manifest Your Son's presence among us.

We humble ourselves before You

and freely confess that we need Your help,

through Jesus Christ our Lord, amen.

QUESTIONS FOR DISCUSSIONS AND STUDY

1. Why does Paul make so much of the church and of church life?

2. Think of two situations each for which the various moral qualities Paul called upon the Colossians to cultivate are relevant. Think of examples of times when Jesus exemplified such qualities in His realtion to others. Examine your heart in light of your findings.

3. Why is personal ambition a negative influence in church life? What does it do and how should its effects be restricted and emended?

4. Discuss the obstacles and the ways to promote Christian unity without compromising the truth.

CHAPTER 8

Living It Out in the Household
(COLOSSIANS 3:18–25)

18 Wives: be submissive to your husbands as is consonant with being in the Lord. 19 Husbands, love your wives and do not be bitter toward them. 20 Children, obey your parents in every way because this is what much pleases the Lord. 21 Fathers, do not frustrate your children, so that they do not lose heart. 22 Slaves, obey in every way your human masters, not just as meets the eye—like those who try to please people—but in heartfelt sincerity—because you fear the Lord. 23 Whatever you do, serve from your heart like you are serving the Lord and not people 24 in the knowledge that from the Lord you will receive the reward of the inheritance. You serve the Lord Jesus Christ. 25 Whoever does wrong will receive the wrong he did, and there is no discrimination.

Paul now moves from general practice to the somewhat more particular. He addresses specific areas of life outside the church, showing how the Colossians were to carry out his exhortation in verse 17 to do "everything in the name of the Lord Jesus, giving thanks to God the Father through him." In the first six verses of the next chapter, Paul continues to speak of the spheres in which the principles of the gospel were to be lived out, so they properly belong to the verses we are about to study in chapter 3. I'm not sure there is wisdom in the present chapter division any more than there was in dividing chapters 2 and 3. For convenience, we will follow the pattern established by the chapter division, but it is important to note the connection between those verses and these that now follow.

Spirituality means living as God would have us live, and doing so willingly because we love God. God is an eternal fellowship of persons: Father, Son, and Holy Spirit. Man, created in the image of God, must live in harmonious fellowship with others. Solitary confinement leads to derangement precisely because this is so. That is why salvation is not exclusively framed in terms of individuals but of communities—churches, families, and nations. In our days the individual is over-emphasized, resulting in the loss of individual identity and an erosion of the value of individuals. There were times when the community was over-emphasized, an emphasis that brought about the same results. The biblical emphasis is on the individual within community and on community as the context in which the individual can find his identity and have real value.

The whole world, all creation, is in view ("the time is coming to gather all nations and tongues, and they shall come and shall see my glory" [Isaiah 66:18]). "Creation itself will be set free from its bondage to corruption and obtain the freedom of the glory of the children of God" (Romans 8:21). Spirituality, then, has to do with how we relate to others, and eschatology has to do with the world adoring God in Christ and submitting to His service. Christians cannot be Christians in isolation; they must live out their salvation in the various spheres of society and in relation to creation, adoring God in Christ and submitting to His service.

The first sphere Paul addresses is the fundamental social context: the family. Human society cannot exist where family life is degraded. The family is the context in which, even in the garden of Eden, man was enabled to find and give the kind of constructive companionship that he needs. How family life is conducted is one of the more important tests of life, a major issue when it comes to the appointment of officers in the church. That is why 1 Timothy 3:1–16 and Titus 1:5–16 point to the family as the primary testing ground of candidates for church office.

"Wives: be submissive to your husbands as is consonant with being in the Lord." Paul's view of marriage is quite non-modern, and lest we excuse ourselves on those grounds, we would do well to remember that they are also contrary to the common views of his day. We've already seen what Paul had to say about slavery, for example. His instructions were not the product of his time and culture; they were framed under inspiration of the Spirit of God and, however countercultural they may be, are binding by virtue of their divine source.

Paul instructs married women to be submissive to their husbands. The biblical requirement is that wives should accept the leadership of their husbands and that they should do so in a dignified manner. There should be no contentions, no effort to subvert, no nagging until one's desire is met. Submission is an expression of a woman's acceptance of the order God has established; it does not make man better or wiser; it simply resolves the issue of who should lead the home.

There is order in the Godhead: The Father initiates, the Son does the will of the Father, and the Spirit glorifies the Father and the Son. Neither is lesser than the other, nor is the glory of either threatened by this order of things. Families and other human societies are to reflect the Godhead in their harmonious love in the context of the order established for their function.

Even in a framework of two there are likely to be disagreements and contrasting viewpoints. Not proceeding until there is unanimity accords each side veto power and can easily paralyze function. God has determined, and legislated through the apostle, that the final word rests with the man as head of the household, who in turn is to answer to God for his decision.

Note that Paul does not instruct husbands to impose their authority over the wives. A wife should never bring her husband to the place in which he is justified in thinking the only way to resolve a disagreement is for him to impose his will. Husbands, on the other hand, should not be too ready to assert their authority, and they should avoid doing so too often. Wives are commanded to be submissive to their husbands; husbands are not instructed to suppress or rule over their wives.

There are areas in which husbands must accord their wives freedom of conscience and maneuver, without thinking that by so doing they are allowing their wives more leeway than is right. A husband who keeps tight control of the family finances and does not allow his wife the latitude to make day-to-day decisions with regard to the family budget is overbearing. A husband who demands of his wife to inform him of every individual she meets, of every conversation she has, of every detail of her routine, and of every penny she spends is suppressing her.

Husbands are to give their wives ample space (and ample reason, as we shall see) for their wives to willingly accept their leadership. They ought not impose it. Marriage is not a dictatorship; it is a covenant of grace and mutual edification. Feminism is right on when it insists that women are equal to men in value. It is dead wrong when it seeks to obliterate differences between men and women or to deny their respective, differing roles. Men are to lead, women to follow. This is God's order, and men and women are to accept their respective roles and seek to fulfill them with loving obedience to the Lord.

It also means women are not to follow their husbands into sin, nor be forced to sin on the grounds of a husband's authority. They must submit to their husband's leadership only as it is consonant with being in the Lord. We learn, then, that there is room for disagreement between spouses. Women and men are to think for themselves, draw their own conclusions, and embrace what they each believe to be true. Women are not to follow their spouses blindly or gullibly. They are as much created in the image of God as are men, and as responsible before their Lord as are their husbands.

Here, too, Jesus is to be preeminent. Women are to relate to their husbands "as is consonant with being in the Lord." Their every action is to be an expression of their love for and obedience to the Lord.

Husbands also have a duty within the family context: "Husbands, love your wives." One would have expected such a requirement to be made of wives—after all, are they not best known for their sacrificial love to the family? That may well be the reason why Paul directed this requirement to husbands, not to wives.

What does it mean to love one's wife? What does it mean to love? "God so loved that he gave" (John 3:16). To love is to emulate God, to exemplify the gospel. To love is to give, above all to give of one's self, and husbands are to give of themselves to their wives. Sacrifice is not only a mother's duty or that of a wife; it is no less a duty of husbands and fathers. To love is to value. The sacrifices love makes are an expression of the value attached to those for whom sacrifice is made.

Husbands are to value their wives, respect them, nurture them, and bear with them the sweet-heavy burden of running a household and bringing up children. It will not do for men to come home after work, change into their slippers, and collapse into the couch with a book, a newspaper' or even the Bible. There are chores to do, dishes to wash, garbage to take out, children to play with, read to, and educate. A man might have had a hard day at the office, but does he even listen when he comes home and says, "Hi, honey, how's your day been?" Does he think of suggesting she go out with her friends in the evening while he stays home and cares for the children? And how about, "Honey, I really appreciate all the hard work you put into being a wife and a mom. In appreciation, I'd like to take you out tonight," or "Why don't you and Cheryl have an evening together?"

To love means to care, to be sensitive, to support. It means a husband provides his wife with opportunities to cultivate her gifts, to relax and to grow as a person. Look again for a moment at the woman described in Proverbs 31. This amazing woman manages the family finances, including investments, plans for the future, preparing for any eventuality while caring for the present, and reaching out to those in need beyond the family circle. She does not have to run to hubby over every detail but has the freedom to make decisions. To no small extent, her husband's success is the fruit of her prowess. She is firm, dignified, wise, and kind. Rather than suppressed, she is a woman worthy of praise (and her husband makes sure to praise her).

Today we often vacillate between foolish male machoism and equally foolish gender indifference. On the one hand, men are encouraged to be cowboy-like, never expressing affection, emotionally detached. They rope and brand cows and tame horses while the women slave in the house and make sure they look pretty when their "man" comes home, slings his pistol on the chair, and sits down to gobble his food, wiping his moustache on the sleeve of his shirt. Women are not cherished; they're used. On the other hand, in some contexts today men are expected to do everything but give birth and suckle while women pursue their more lucrative career. Such "men" aren't men—they're hamstrung males.

Loving means protecting, and a man has to be strong to be able to protect his wife because there will be many things that will threaten her: the changes involved in marriage, missing her parents, siblings, and friends, financial responsibilities, the monthly period, bearing a child, gaining weight, suckling, sleepless nights, having to cope with the children, cleaning the house, shopping and cooking for the family, entertaining guests, supporting her husband, disciplining the children (Let's see how unfazed YOU are after a solid day with the kids), looking nice for church, doing the laundry, painting the hallway, tending the garden … and being pleasant when his majesty Mr. Breadwinner comes home from work. There will be times when she will be tired beyond words, and if her husband is not sensitive, he will never notice. Loving means making a point of noticing, and responding lovingly and protectively when there is need.

I don't hug my wife enough. I don't tell her as often as I should that I love her. Even as I write, Bracha is out buying shoes. I should have offered to go with her. It's not that I'd enjoy going shopping, trying on an endless array of shoes, and finally returning to the first shop we visited to make a purchase; it's that Bracha would enjoy me showing more interest in her and in what she is doing.

Loving is the way to earn the right to be followed. Loving is the moral basis of a husband's leadership role. I need to do better. If you are a husband, do you?

Did you notice that little phrase at the end of what Paul has to say to husbands? "Do not be bitter toward them." Do not allow a root of bitterness to develop between you, gnaw at your relationship, and destroy it. If there is an issue to discuss, do not let the sun set on your anger. Talk it over; pray together about it. Manage your disagreements as befits Christians. Love your wives, give them space, and lead, above all, by example. Win them by your love and remember: there is no room in the family for the kind of elitism to which the Colossian Christians were encouraged to aspire.

Next come the children: "Children, obey your parents in every way because this is what much pleases the Lord." The Greek actually uses a word most commonly translated "fathers," but was frequently used to denote parents (see, for example, Hebrews 9:23). That seems to be the meaning here.

The children's chief duty toward their parents has to do with obedience. Parents should not bribe their children into doing what they are told, nor should children be terrified into doing so. They should be taught that obedience is their duty before God. Parents are not always right, but they are always to be obeyed "in every way"; that is to say, not only by doing what they are told, but by doing it willingly, from the heart, "because this is what much pleases the Lord." Obedience to one's parents is part and parcel with obedience to God. It is a spiritual act, an act of worship.

There is a certain order in the universe, with God in Christ paramount. A time will come when children will have the duty and the right to educate their own children. That is when they can call the shots. But as long as they are minors, their safety is to be found in accepting the thoughtful, godly, loving guidance of their parents.

Such an order lays a tremendous burden on parents, especially fathers: "Fathers, do not frustrate your children, so that they do not lose heart." What frustrates children more than anything else? What causes them to loose heart? Inconsistency on the part of parents, lack of fairness, unfulfilled warnings, arbitrariness, contempt, and suppression all contribute to a child's frustration and lead to the kind of indifference that expresses despair.

Children are taught to lie by parents who break promises and do not carry out warnings. They develop a well-justified sense of injustice if their parents do not hear them out before reacting, treat any of their siblings differently, or vacillate between forbidding and allowing the same kind of behavior. They are frustrated when they do not know what to expect, because their parents' reaction depends more on the parents' mood than on what they have done. They rebel or sink into indifference if their parents do not respect the image of God in them and therefore suppress initiative, repeatedly express lack of confidence in them, or do not encourage them to think and act on their own. If the children can never do right, why should they try? What is the point of trying when there is never any encouragement if, however well the child performs or however much he or she has invested effort, no compliment will be forthcoming? If they can never meet the standard, they will inevitably despair. Trust your child. Give her opportunity to grow, to make mistakes and learn from them, to develop her own God-given propensities, to be herself.

Contrary to what Roman culture taught, children are not subject to the arbitrary whims of their parents. Nor are they extensions of the parents' persona. Parents are not to live out their unfulfilled ambitions through their children, nor impose their views—not even their faith. True faith is the product of a work of God in the human heart, not the imposition of man. It is the God-given response of an individual to God; it can never be forced by human hands. If we are to avoid frustrating our children and causing them to lose heart, we must educate them to think independently and equip them with spiritual and moral standards. Such standards are best inculcated by way of example. Children who grow up in a godly home where faithful, tender affection is expressed, integrity is preserved, and God is lovingly feared will have the means to weigh and make their own decisions. God will draw to Himself those among our children whom He sees fit.

The opposite of frustration and loss of heart is what we should seek for our children: a holy, humble, honest ambition to fully realize their gifts; a respectful, caring attitude toward others; a sense of dignified integrity, vigor, and happiness. When these are combined with God's saving, sanctifying grace, our children will realize their full potential, and God will be glorified in them. What more could we desire?

False teachers were encouraging the Colossians to despise weakness and lay claim to a mystical knowledge that lifted one above the level of common individuals. The gospel teaches us that we are to respect and love all, and to treat others as equals, regardless of our respective roles.

Speaking of respect, one of the most remarkable examples of how the gospel transforms a culture is found in its application to the relationship between owner and slave. Roman life was largely based on slavery. There were more slaves in Rome than there were citizens. Slaves, procured primarily as the consequence of war, were considered to be mere possessions, to be used and disposed of at their owners' will. The gospel did not challenge Roman slavery directly; it undermined it by putting slaves and slave owners on the same level, treating them as equal objects of God's grace and judgment, and laying a solidly spiritual basis for the slaves' relationship to their owners:

> Slaves, obey in every way your human masters, not just as meets the eye—like those who try to please people—but in heartfelt sincerity—because you fear the Lord. Whatever you do, serve from your heart like you are serving the Lord and not people in the knowledge that from the Lord you will receive the reward of the inheritance. You serve the Lord Jesus Christ. Whoever does wrong will receive the wrong he did, and there is no discrimination.

Coming from the pen of a man who grew up in a first-century Roman city (Tarsus was just that, although situated in what we would now call south eastern Turkey), these are quite remarkable statements. Slaves were enjoined to obey their human masters, but for reasons an average Roman would not expect. The term used to describe the obedience slaves are to give their masters is exactly the term the apostle used to describe the kind of obedience children are to render their parents: "in every way."

He then goes on to explain: "Not just as meets the eye—like those who try to please people—but in heartfelt sincerity—because you fear the Lord. Whatever you do, serve from your heart like you are serving the Lord and not people in the knowledge that from the Lord you will receive the reward of the inheritance. You serve the Lord Jesus Christ." In other words, view whatever you are called upon to do in the context of your slavery in terms of worship. Serve the Lord in the way you serve your masters while tending their flocks, farming their fields, cleaning their homes, or educating their children. Paul repeated this statement three times in the course of these short encouragements.

It does not matter what we do—sew a button, mow the lawn, build a house, trade in stocks, sell merchandise, or whatever other activity in which life involves us—everything should be an act of worship and, because of that, done to the best of our ability. In the final run, we are serving the Lord, and we should do so from the heart, eagerly, sincerely, and happily. We're not working for praise, a salary, or just because we must, but in the knowledge that "from the Lord [we] will receive the reward of the inheritance."

Our reward is not to be found in the passing advantages humans can give us. Our reward is of infinitely greater value; it is "the reward of the inheritance" of which Paul spoke in 1:12. Slaves are equal recipients of that inheritance, and "whoever does wrong," regardless of whether he is a Jew or a Gentile, a freeman or a slave, "will receive the wrong he did, and there is no discrimination." On the Day of Judgment, God will not take one's social standing into account. He will not inquire as to our race or gender, our education or personal background, how many times we fasted or attended a Passover Seder. "Whoever does wrong" will be punished. Slave owners will stand at the bar of divine judgment on the same level as their slaves, and both will have to give account of themselves: 'Did you treat your slaves with respect and equal justice?' 'Did you serve your master heartily, as one serving the Lord?'

This is a promise and an encouragement to slaves, often mistreated by their owners: be patient and do your work in confident hope because the Judgment Day will undoubtedly come and justice will be served. It is also a warning to those who owned slaves: if you do not wish to receive the wrong you imposed on others, you had better treat your slaves with respect, care for their needs, and employ them in a just, gracious manner.

Paul's closing words concerning judgment and the lack of partiality in judgment are similar to what the apostle had to say in Romans 2:6–11, where he stated that God

> will render to each one according to his works: to those who by patience in well-doing seek for glory and honor and immortality, he will give eternal life; but for those who are self-seeking and do not obey the truth, but obey unrighteousness, there will be wrath and fury. There will be tribulation and distress for every human being

who does evil, the Jew first and also the Greek, but glory and honor
and peace for everyone who does good, the Jew first and also the
Greek. For God shows no partiality.

Here is a truth, variously applied in differing contexts, relevant to them
both.

If this principle is true with regard to slaves and their masters, it is
all the truer with regard to employees and their employers, hired hands
and those who hire them. Both those who provide services and those
who pay for them should treat each other in the fear of God, giving at
least as much as they contracted to give in terms of performance and
remuneration.

LET'S SUMMARIZE

- Salvation has to do with more than the individual. All creation and
  all human society are in view. The more we understand this, the
  more consistently we will be enabled to live by the gospel.

- God has established order in society. Living in accordance with
  that order is an expression of our love for God in the context of
  daily reality. Such order does not imply inferiority. It reflects the
  wonder of the Godhead.

- Wives are to accept their husband's leadership, and husbands are
  to be worthy of such a role by their sacrificial love for their wives.
  Children are to honor God by obeying their parents, and parents
  are to respect and cultivate their children, above all by personal example. Slaves are to serve God in their labor for their owners, and
  slave owners are to treat their slaves with respect, as we will see in
  the next chapter.

LET'S PRAY

God of all glory,

Father, Son, and Holy Spirit,

three in one and one in three;

distinct yet one without dissensions;

one yet without suppressions;

an eternal, harmonious, holy, happy God.

We are called into community to serve You

and reflect the beauty of Your harmony as we live together.

Give us grace so that You might have glory through us

and the world might know You have sent Your Son to save,

in Jesus' name, amen.

QUESTIONS FOR DISCUSSION AND STUDY

1. Discuss practical ways wives and husbands, children and parents can fulfill their God-given roles. What is the extent and what are the limits of their duties? How can they reflect the Godhead in the specific circumstances you discuss?

2. Discuss the impact of such family life on the world around us.

3. In what way can family life as called for by Paul give hope? What is the relationship between such family life and eschatology?

4. Note that the gospel establishes duties rather than granting rights and privileges. Discuss the practical implications of this approach and compare these with the practical implications that would result if the gospel accorded rights. Which approach is closer to the norm established today in society? Draw conclusions.

CHAPTER 9

Closing Words
(COLOSSIANS 4:1–6)

1 You masters, provide justice and equality to your slaves in the knowledge that you too have a Master in heaven.

2 Continue in your prayers, be alert as you pray, giving thanks, 3 praying also together with us that God would open to us a door for the message, to declare the mystery of the Christ, for which I have also been bound, 4 so that I might reveal it as I ought to speak.

5 Conduct yourselves wisely toward those outside, making the most of the time. 6 Your speech should always be gracious, having been seasoned with salt so you know how to answer each person.

As already stated, these verses properly belong to the previous chapter, especially the first verse. It seems to me it would have been more appropriate to divide the chapters at verse 7.

Having provided instructions as to how to implement the principles he laid down in 1:1–3:17 by addressing the family (wives, husbands, children, and parents), the apostle turns to the wider Roman-era household, which would often include slaves and slave owners. At the end of chapter 3, he spoke of the duties of slaves. Here he turns to speak of their master-owners (v. 1), and then to the conduct of the church (vv. 2–6). Finally, in the following section, he concludes his letter with a series of greetings, short instructions and a signature.

"You masters, provide justice and equality to your slaves in the knowledge that you too have a Master in heaven." At the end of chapter 3, Paul placed slaves and slave owners on the same level by according the slaves the same moral value. He closed by intimating that all will be subject to judgment. Now he levels them again by explicitly submitting them both to the lordship of Christ. Slave owners are to honor God by respecting their slaves.

Masters are required to treat their slaves justly. According to Roman law, slaves had no legal standing. They could be fed or starved, pampered or beaten, killed or be kept alive at will. They were disposable property. There were some cases in which slaves rose to great power, or in which nobles emancipated and even adopted slaves, according them equal or higher status than their own children. But this too was contingent on the whim and wish of the owners. Slaves could not appeal for justice. Their only hope was mercy.

Paul places slaves and their owners before the bar of God's justice because they were both created in the image of God. He requires masters to recognize that their slaves are human beings, as much objects of God's grace and love as any. Under inspiration of the Spirit of God, he imposes on slave-owners duties with regard to their slaves.

If that was not clear enough, Paul makes it doubly clear by instructing masters to provide their slaves with "equality" in the recognitions that they too "have a Master in heaven." In other words, in a real sense they are fellow-slaves, and will have to give account to their heavenly Master as to how they have treated their equals.

Such statements were nothing short of revolutionary. To the extent that the words were understood, they destroyed the grounds on which the institution of slavery was based. No man has arbitrary rights over another. No man may purchase or sell another. No man may treat his fellow as if he were mere property. Justice and equality are to reign. This is one of the ways in which gospel principles overturn social mores and lay the basis for a moral, kind, respectful society. No other religion has done that. No other religion can.

Elitism, promoted by the Colossian heretics, ultimately asserts that one person is of greater value than another and lays the grounds for a worldview that permits slavery. Nazism was but another expression of that kind of elitism, and another is totalitarian communism. Nazis and Communists considered themselves the cream of humanity, the highest stage in an evolutionary process. They were, therefore, accorded privileges denied to others.

The household, the church, and society are the spheres in which we Christians live out our lives. They are the spheres in which the gospel is to be exemplified in the course of daily dealings. Paul had already dealt with the family. In verses 2–4, he addressed the church on an important aspect of its internal life and then, in verses 5–7, on its conduct in society. It is significant to note that most of what Paul had said up to this point has immediate relevancy to church life.

Churches (and Christian families) should be praying communities. This is so obvious that Paul does not exhort the Colossians to pray; instead he says, "Continue in your prayers," assuming they prayed as a matter of course. Prayer should be the natural, frequent activity of church life. "Be alert [as you pray]," Paul exhorts. Don't let your thoughts wander, and be ready to turn anything you hear into a subject for prayer. Often, when an individual prays in public, those who hear him simply wait until it is time to say "amen" without really entering into the content of the prayer. "Be alert" means that we not only listen to the contents of the prayer being offered but that we engage our hearts and minds in it as well. Contrary to the practice of some, there is room for an occasional "amen," "yes, Lord," and "hallelujah" as we are led in prayer.

Did you notice the term just used "as we are led in prayer"? If one is leading, others are expected to follow. That is the very least of what I think Paul means when he called on the Colossians to be alert as they continued to pray. One led, but all prayed; one voiced the praise, confession, and requests of all, while all identified with the prayer by sharing in it.

Paul exhorts, "Be alert as you pray." How many of us need this simple reminder? How alert are we when all bow their heads in prayer? Do our thoughts wander? Do we doze off? Or do we truly participate in the prayers being offered by listening to them actively and joining our hearts with the praise, confession, and requests made?

Prayer should always involve "giving thanks." Praise and gratitude are the inevitable consequences of understanding the gospel. There is so much for which we ought to be thankful. God loads us daily with benefits seen and unseen. He watches over us with tender care. He has done so much for us by revealing Himself to us and drawing us to Himself.

We are too quick to submit our requests, too selfish to be as grateful as we ought to be. Once we've met the required standard of verbal gratitude and praise, we hurry to the real business of prayer, the submitting of our requests before God. Christian prayer should always be engaged in honest thankfulness. Nothing we have has been deserved; it is all a gift of grace. The food we eat, the air we breathe, the soil on which we walk, the world in which we live, the rain and the sunshine, our parents, spouses, children, and friends, the lovely breakfast and the beautiful landscape— these and more are all gifts of God. We should "be thankful."

Next, Paul seeks the support of the Colossians for himself: "Praying also together with us that God would open to us a door for the message." Although an apostle, he does not consider himself perfect or one of the elite. He needs the prayerful support of all God's saints.

What is his concern? Why does he ask the Colossians to pray? Were they to bring to God the story of Aunt Emma's thyroid or Uncle Jim's back pain? How about Bill's search for employment, Corrie's troubled pregnancy, or Jacky's choice of education? These all are, of course, important topics. They affect our lives deeply. But Paul's concerns are for issues that affect our lives even more deeply. Pray, Paul says, "God would open to us a door for the message." Paul is under detention, liable to lose his life. Yet he does not ask to be spared, or for his needs to be met while under house arrest. He teaches us by example not to focus so much on our needs or on matters related to earthly things. We are to lift our eyes and look beyond our needs and those of the circle of our friends and family.

We are to think of the gospel, of the glory of God, of the extension of His kingdom, of the salvation of souls and the health of the church. Pray "God would open to us a door for the message." Of course, the message has to do in this case with "the mystery of Christ," and Paul's desire is "to declare" that mystery. As noted earlier, Paul has described the mystery in 1:26–27, it is summarized in 1:27 as "Christ among you, the hope for the glory," referring to the ultimate, eternal unity of redeemed humanity, presently realized to a significant extent in the church.

Paul is asking the Colossians to help him through prayer to promote the very unity that was threatened by the heretical teaching offered in their city. He assumes that, like him, the Colossians were thrilled at the wonder of the mystery and would embrace it fondly, as he does. He assumes their commitment to the sufficiency of Christ and to the unity of all who confess Christ's name and revel in his achievements.

"For which mystery I have also been bound." This is a reference to the detention imposed on Paul, first in a Roman prison in Caesarea and then under house arrest in Rome. Had he kept to "the simple gospel" and not opposed those who insisted Jewish traditional practices should be added to one's faith in Christ, he would not have been arrested. Nor would he have found it necessary to demand he be tried in Rome, before Caesar. Paul was arrested because he insisted on preaching the mystery and seeking support to help ensure he would "reveal" that mystery in his preaching and in the mixed composition, setup, and function of the churches God used him to establish.

Not trusting himself, Paul now seeks prayer from others to help ensure he would speak of that mystery "as I ought to speak": with boldness, exuberance, and eager expectation. He does not trust himself to be faithful. Like us, Paul desires to be liked and accepted. But he desires above all to please and glorify God. He therefore asks the Colossians to pray he would overcome his reticence, conquer his fears, and speak out for the truth of the gospel, the unity of the church, and the sufficiency of Christ in a way these topics deserved. As human as any of us, Paul knows he needs God's help to live that way, and he asks for such help.

Finally, he refers briefly to the church's conduct in relation to the world: "Conduct yourselves wisely toward those outside." Wise conduct is the product of thought, relating of principle to precept, and precept to duty. This is one of the more appealing characteristics of the Faith of the gospel: Christian conduct is not based on arbitrary precept; it encourages thought—not mystical experimentation, not existential experience, but a conscious effort to understand the world, and to subdue and harness it to the achievement of its divinely appointed goal. The Christian Faith is an extrapolation of the Creator's command to Adam, to serve Him by acting as His agent on earth subduing, filling, and ruling over it in God's name.

"Those outside" are not the common Christians, content with Christ and indifferent to the higher spiritual plane to which the heretics invited the Colossians; they are non-Christians, people who are not consciously and willingly enlisted in the service of God and who therefore remain outside the pale of His saving blessings. They are separated from Christ, outside the church, outside the covenant, and outside the fellowship of the saints, without God and without hope in the world.

Wisdom dictates that Christians conduct themselves in such a way as to implement the principles of the gospel in ways that will challenge these outsiders and convey the gospel to them. A morality grounded on, framed, and motivated by the fear of God and that treasures holiness more than profit is an example of such wisdom. A humility that issues out of the biblical view of man and a generosity that is the product of God's grace and kindness are further such examples.

Christians should exemplify the gospel in their daily lives, in how they use their time, energies, and possessions, in how they drive, choose their careers, educate their children, and make decisions. They should be engaged in the study of God's Word and in thinking deeply about the world in terms of the Faith. Their light should shine in such a fashion that it points onlookers to God and moves them to worship Him.

One aspect of living wisely has to do with what Paul describes as "making the most of the time," literally, "redeeming" the time, and I might well have chosen to translate the word *time* as "opportunity." Note the definite article. Paul was not speaking of time in general but of a specific time. There are two words in Greek we might translate as "time." One is *chronos*, which means time in general. The other is *kairos*, which refers to a specific moment in time, often an opportune moment. The word Paul uses here is *kairos*.

This immediately brings us back to the apostle's exhortation that the Colossians were to conduct themselves wisely. Guided by principle and fortified by wisdom, they were to discern the implications of every moment and make the most of each to live consistent with the gospel and, in this way, proclaim the gospel by their lives. As noted earlier, this was one of the most compelling features of the early church.

Another aspect of living wisely is indicated by Paul when he says, "Your speech should always be gracious, having been seasoned with salt so you know how to answer each person." Salt purifies. It also adds something of a gentle sting to food, rendering it more palatable. The simile of seasoning our speech with salt would indicate a soft, pure attitude, void of rancor and unkind or unclean expressions, rendering what we have to say, however stark, more palatable than the angry words we are often inclined to employ.

Wisdom would further dictate that our answer is formulated in a way that takes into account the individual being addressed. While always respectful, we are not expected to address our spouse or our boss in the same way we are expected to address our children. Nor ought we address our spouse at a moment of aggravation as we might legitimately do in a calmer situation. In all aspects and in all the walks of life, we are to live out the gospel, demonstrating the holiness and the grace of God in ways that those who watch us discover the validity and beauty of God's message and see the validity of a life lived out for God.

LET'S SUMMARIZE

- The gospel transforms society by calling it to God and to godliness. Slavery was first transformed and then dismantled by the gospel.

- There is no room for elitism in society, the church, or the family. We are all truly equal and should treat each other as such.

- Prayer is necessary to church and family life. Prayer should express our sense of priorities by putting God first: thanking Him and seeking His glory in all things before requesting anything for ourselves or for those close to us.

- We must both pray and labor for unity in the family, church, and society. We should pray that those who preach will be enabled to be faithful and that God would encourage them in their task.

- We must live wisely. To do so, we must think as deeply and as carefully as we can about the gospel.

- We must make maximal use of our time and every opportunity.

- We must watch the use of our tongues.

LET'S PRAY

Glorious God,

we thank you for the power of the gospel to transform,

for its beauty and wisdom,

and for the subtle way it often works.

Teach us to understand the gospel.

Show us its inner workings,

the motivations it creates,

and the goals it establishes.

Make these our own.

Teach us to think, and to think as Christians

ever seeking to serve and honor You,

so that the gospel shapes our lives

and our lives commend the gospel.

Teach us to love and respect all of our fellow humans,

to make best use of our time and of our tongues,

and to grow in holiness as we go through life.

Cleanse us of our sins and protect us from temptation.

Bring us to Your eternal home,

that we may love You purely, as we ought.

We seek Your grace in Jesus' name, amen.

QUESTIONS FOR DISCUSSION AND STUDY

1. Consider the baneful way elitism invades various spheres of life and how it has impacted human history. Apply your findings to your own family, church, and social life. What do you need to change?

2. Measure your prayer life by Paul's example and think of practical ways you can improve your prayers.

3. Discuss practical ways that thinking rightly made a positive contribution to life. Consider ways to encourage and equip Christian thinking in the various spheres of life.

CHAPTER 10

Greetings and Practicalities
(COLOSSIANS 4:7–18)

7 About me Tychicus, the beloved brother and faithful servant and fellow-slave in the Lord, will inform you, 8 whom I sent to you for this very purpose, so that you might know the things concerning us and that he might comfort your hearts 9 with Onesimus, the faithful and beloved brother who belongs to you. They will inform you of the situation here.

10 Aristarchus my fellow-prisoner, greets you, and Mark, Barnabas's cousin (about whom you received instructions: if he comes to you receive him), 11 and Jesus who has been names Justus— these are the only fellow-workers in the kingdom of God from among the circumcised who became a comfort to me. 12 Epaphras who belongs to you, a slave of Christ Jesus, is always struggling for you in his prayers so that you might stand complete and having been assured in all the will of God, 13 because I testify concerning him that he is very concerned for you and those in Laodicea and those in Hierapolis.

14 Luke the beloved physician greets you, and Demas. 15 Greet the brothers in Laodicea, and Nympha and those of the church in her house, 16 and whenever this letter is read to you, see that it is also read in the church of the Laodiceans so that you also read the letter to those in Laodicea, 17 and tell Archippus, "take care of

the service which you have received from the Lord, so you carry it out."

18 Greetings in my handwriting, from Paul. Remember my captivity. Grace be with you.

Paul closes with the promise that Tychicus and Onesimus, the bearers of this letter, would provide the Colossians with up-to-date information concerning his situation. He then proceeds with a series of greetings from Christians who were with him in Rome, coupled with his personal greetings and brief exhortations. Finally, he attaches his signature. With the exception of Justus, all individuals mentioned here are also mentioned in Paul's letter to Philemon.

"About me Tychicus, the beloved brother and faithful servant and fellow-slave in the Lord, will inform you, whom I sent to you for this very purpose, so that you might know the things concerning us and that he might comfort your hearts with Onesimus, the faithful and beloved brother who belongs to you. They will inform you of the situation here." Let's pause for a moment and introduce the individuals mentioned in these verses.

Tychicus, described by Luke as an Asian (Acts 20:4), hailed from the Roman administrative region of Asia, presently in western Turkey, where Troas, Colossae Hierapolis, and the seven churches mentioned in Revelation 2 and 3 were situated. He is first mentioned as a member of Paul's party when the apostle traveled through Greece and Macedonia on his way to Jerusalem with a collection from the churches among the Gentiles for the brethren in Jerusalem, impoverished by a drought that decimated the Roman world of the time.

Tychicus was with Paul in Rome. He seemed to have been with the apostle throughout the latter's two-year detention in Caesarea, traveled with him to Rome, and was sent out by him, with Onesimus, bearing this letter, one to Philemon, and the letter to the Ephesians (Ephesians 6:21–22). Apparently, he also carried one to the Laodiceans (Colossians 4:15–16), which may have been a copy of Paul's letter to the Ephesians.

Paul was released following Caesar's decision and continued to travel for the gospel. From 2 Timothy 4:12 and Titus 3:12 we learn that Tychicus rejoined the apostle's company and was sent by him to Crete to replace Titus. He was with Paul again during the apostle's second and last imprisonment in Rome, during which time he was sent by the apostle to Ephesus to replace Timothy. Some believe Tychicus is the brother spoken of in 2 Corinthians 8:22: "Our brother whom we have often tested and found earnest in many matters, but who is now more earnest than ever because of his great confidence in you." If they are correct, then another of Tychicus' missions was to the troubled church in Corinth.

In this letter Paul described him as a "beloved brother and faithful servant and fellow-slave in the Lord." Paul was, as discussed earlier, an affectionate man. But he did not hand out compliments lightly; he had high standards, and Tychicus met them. He was "faithful," proving himself a "fellow-slave in the Lord," and thereby became particularly beloved to Paul. Unlike many who take every advantage to intimate how far advanced they consider themselves to be in comparison with others, Paul put Tychicus on his level—a fellow-slave, an equal partner. We lead best when we focus on encouraging others. Paul knew this well and devoted a good deal of his energies to encouraging and promoting others to areas of responsibility. We could well learn from him.

He "will inform you, whom I sent to you for this very purpose, so that you might know the things concerning us and that he might comfort your hearts." Paul's relations with the churches and with the people alongside whom he worked were not exclusively based on authority but on mutual affection and a shared commitment to the Lord. Paul knew that the Colossians would be concerned for him and would want to learn of his welfare and his labors. He considered himself obliged to report to them. In spite of his strong personality, the apostle was not a loose cannon; he was an emissary of the churches, including those he founded. He reported to them. And his relations with the churches were not merely formal; they were affectionately personal.

Onesimus is mentioned next here (Colossians 4:9) and in the letter to Philemon, a prominent member of the church in Colossae and, most likely, the one in whose home the church met. Onesimus was one of Philemon's slaves. He fled to Rome after robbing his master, met Paul, and was converted (Philemon v. 10). The apostle sent him back to his duties as a slave in Philemon's household (Philemon v. 12), which is what occasioned his letter to Philemon. Nothing more is known of Onesimus. Tradition seeks to fill in the blanks but nothing is certain.

Onesimus was not engaged in gospel work, but he, like Tychicus, is described as a "faithful and beloved brother, who belongs to you [that is, he came from Colossae]. They [Tychicus and Onesimus] will inform you of the situation here." Although a young Christian, Onesimus was entrusted with a mission, to be carried out in fellowship with the elder, more experienced Tychicus: to report to the church in Colossae. The fact that he was a slave—and a runaway slave who probably stole from his owner (Philemon v. 18)—did not alter Paul's confidence in him. He had been converted. He had repented of his sins and was now on his way back to his owner, where he would have to accept Philemon's decision as to the consequences of his actions—and slave-owners had a life-or-death power over their slaves.

There is an important lesson here for each of us. We do not like to bear responsibility for our deeds, but repentance is never merely verbal; it involves owning up and, where possible, restitution. It means being willing to bear the punishment due to us for our sins.

Paul then mentions Aristarchus, whom he describes as "my fellow-prisoner" here and in the letter to Philemon as his "fellow soldier" (v. 2). We first met him as a member of Paul's party in Ephesus (Acts 19:29), on which occasion he was described as a Macedonian (Ephesus was in Asia; Macedonia in what is now northern Greece). Acts 2:4 and 27:2 pinpoint his city of residence, indicating that he was a Thessalonian (another Macedonian city). From Colossians 4:10–11 we learn that he was Jewish.

Paul conveys greetings from Aristarchus, with whom, it is reasonable to deduce, the Colossians were acquainted or at least that they had heard of him. Aristarchus traveled ahead of Paul from Ephesus to Troas, where he awaited the apostle (Acts 20:1–4). He appears next alongside Paul on the trip from Caesarea to Rome (Acts 27:2), and then in the letters to Colossians and to Philemon, written from Rome in the course of Paul's first detention. He is not mentioned elsewhere in the New Testament.

The next individual to be referenced is "Mark, Barnabas's cousin." This is John Mark, mentioned in Acts 12:12, whose mother hosted the church in Jerusalem and to which home Peter went when he was miraculously released from prison. Mark then appeared in Antioch, in the company of his uncle, Barnabas, and Paul. He accompanied the two at the beginning of their first missionary endeavor (Acts 13:1–5) and then left them, rather abruptly.

In the course of that initial outreach we read, "Paul and his companions set sail from Paphos and came to Perga in Pamphylia, and Mark left them and returned to Jerusalem" (Acts 13:13). Later, in Acts 15:37–39, we learn that when Paul and Barnabas considered a second missionary endeavor:

> Barnabas wanted to take with them John called Mark. But Paul
> thought best not to take with them one who had withdrawn from
> them in Pamphylia and had not gone with them to the work. And
> there arose a sharp disagreement, so that they separated from each
> other. Barnabas took Mark with him and sailed away to Cyprus, but
> Paul chose Silas and departed, having been commended by the
> brothers to the grace of the Lord.

Apparently Paul viewed Mark's departure as a kind of desertion.

In light of the fact that Mark returned from Pamphylia to Jerusalem—not to Antioch, from whence he had been sent—and from Luke's
emphasis on Paul and Barnabas's focus on the Gentiles (Acts 14:26–27),
it is reasonable to conclude Mark was uncomfortable with this focus. He
therefore left the two and made his way to Jerusalem, assuming he would
find support for his views there. We do know that Paul later met with
opposition in Jerusalem, including a measure of suspicion from fellow
Jewish Christians. It was while seeking to accommodate them that he
was arrested in the temple court.

Whatever might have been the reason for Mark's departure and
Paul's displeasure with him, by the time the letter to the Colossians was
written, the two had reconciled. From what Paul has to say about him
here we conclude that Mark had a change of heart. He came to understand the truth of the apostle's insistence on the unity of the church,
incorporating Jews and Gentiles, as Mark is described as one of the few
Jewish Christians who shared in Paul's efforts (my "fellow-workers in
the kingdom of God from among the circumcised who became a comfort to me."). Obviously he underwent a complete turn-around. When
Paul wrote to Timothy during his second detention in Rome, the two had
clearly developed an affectionate camaraderie (2 Timothy 4:11).

Mark, then, was a man of principle, but he loved God's truth more
than he loved his version of it. He was capable of changing his mind and
seeking amends with those whose views he had earlier taken to task. And
Paul was not vindictive. He harbored no ill will toward Mark and had
enough grace in his heart to recognize that people can change.

Paul says regarding Mark, "About whom you received instructions: if
he comes to you receive him." We learn, then, that there was meaningful cooperation between the two. Paul not only knew of Mark's intended
movements but supported them.

Most scholars identify John Mark with the Mark who wrote the gospel called by his name, most likely on the basis of Peter's narrative.

After Mark comes "Jesus, who has been named Justus." Nothing is known of Justus apart from what is written here. He, Mark, and Aristarchus were Jewish Christians ("those of the circumcision" Colossians 4:11) whom Paul described as his "only fellow-workers in the kingdom of God from among the circumcised who became a comfort to me." The note of sadness in the apostle's voice is evident. He was human. He longed like all of us for understanding, recognition, appreciation, and friendship.

Paul felt very much alone because of his commitment to the evangelization of the Gentiles and the unity of the church. Still, he was willing to pay the price as long as he could continue in the work to which Christ had called him through the Holy Spirit, "to carry my name before the Gentiles and kings and the children of Israel" (Acts 9:15). What is more, he was shown in advance "how much he must suffer for the sake of my name" (Acts 9:16), yet he took on the task committed to him. Recalling that Paul wrote to the Colossian Christians while in detention in Rome, the fact that only these three stood by Paul and shared his labors at the time speaks poorly for the brethren who made up the church in Rome. Their proximity only served to enhance Paul's sense of loneliness. God forbid that we be like them.

The servants of God are called to tread a painful path. Loneliness is but one aspect of the pain they must endure. Such men are often considered, much as we tend to consider Paul, to be above the emotional wear and tear normal humans experience. They are thought of as never afraid, never offended, never in need of a sympathetic hand of understanding and comfort. Not a few collapse under the burden of such a calling, especially if they were taught to expect the opposite or if they do not know how to derive strength from the Lord. Paul sensed the hurt. But he persisted because he lived and breathed, preached and suffered for the Son of God, who loved him and gave Himself for him. Paul was dead to the world, not in the sense that it had no appeal to him, but in the sense that he loved Christ more.

We should not think those who serve us are beyond human feelings. Leadership is a lonely calling, requiring tremendous emotional sacrifice. Let's be sensitive to those who serve us and support them as best we can. Let's seek to be their comfort and encouragement rather than add to their burdens. When they stumble, let's be quick to help them back onto their feet. Above all, let's pray much for them.

Justus is followed by Epaphras. As noted when we looked at Colossians 1:7, although Epaphras is an abbreviated form of Epaphroditus, this Epaphras is not the Epaphroditus mentioned in Paul's letter to the Philippians. The latter was a resident of the city of Philippi and associated with the church there (Philippians 2:26; 3:18). The Colossian Epaphras was the one through whom the Colossians had first heard the gospel, and who harbored a spiritual interest in the three churches in the Lycean Valley.

As Paul puts it, "I testify concerning him that he is very concerned for you and those in Laodicea and those in Hierapolis." We do not know why such a testimony was needed, but apparently it was. The early church was not free of the human weaknesses that dog every community. We expect too much of the church when we demand that it be perfect in the here and now. How could it be so as long as we, and others like us, belong? What should characterize the church on earth is not the absence of human failings but the way these are dealt with and the corporate striving to forgive each other and to overcome those failings for God's sake.

Epaphras is Paul's "a slave of Christ Jesus," also described in 1:7 as "a faithful servant of Christ." Epaphras' interest in the churches of Colossae, Hierapolis, and Laodicea motivated him to engage in earnest prayer. Epaphras is said to be "always struggling for you in his prayers so that you might stand complete and having been assured in all the will of God." That is how we should pray: struggling. Always. That is what we should be struggling for: "that you might stand complete and having been assured in all the will of God."

The will of God spoken of here is not an abstraction. Neither is it God's hidden, personal will for each one of us as individuals. It is, rather, the will of God as expressed, defended, and insisted upon in this letter and to which Paul referred in 1:9 as a humble awareness of our incapacities and of Christ's glorious sufficiency; a leaning on His achievements rather than anything we might do; a recognition that none of us will ever better another in Christ—that we are all equal and that we must live as equals rather than striving to prove ourselves on a higher level; a love that bears and forbears because it recognizes that we were called to serve God in one body; a love that unites all who are in Christ in the bond of peace, refuses to submit to human traditions, and accords Christ the sufficiency that is rightly His.

Luke is next. Lukas in Greek is an abbreviation of Lukanos. He was the composer of the Gospel of Luke and the book of Acts, and a physician by trade. From the fact that Paul said that only Aristarchus, Justus and Mark among those with him were Jewish, we conclude that Luke was not. Since certain sections of Acts were written in the first person plural (we), we conclude that Luke was a witness to many of the events narrated in that book. Like John, who refrains from mentioning himself in his Gospel, Luke did not name himself in the book of Acts. His humility is exemplary.

On the other hand, Luke excluded himself from the circle of "those who from the beginning were eyewitnesses and ministers of the word" (Luke 1:2), and "who delivered a narrative of those events to us" (Luke 1:1–2). He was not a witness to the events described in his Gospel. Rather, he examined "all things closely for some time past" (Luke 1:3) and then chose to write.

Luke's introduction to the Gospel that bears his name is a more formal classical Greek than any other portion of the New Testament. The fact that he chose to write the rest of his Gospel in a Greek that reflected the spoken language of Galilee and Judea is evidence of his excellent education and his literary skill.

Following the indications supplied by the use of "we" in Acts we see that Luke first associated with Paul in Troas, immediately following Paul's vision of a Macedonian calling the apostle to cross the straits: "Immediately we sought to go on into Macedonia, concluding God had called us to preach the gospel to them" (Acts 16:10). Some have surmised Luke was a Macedonian who met Paul, heard the gospel from him, and pleaded with him to preach the gospel in his homeland, Macedonia. Following that conversation or prior to it, Paul saw Luke in a dream and heard his plea.

Paul crossed the straits accompanied by Luke and others and, upon preaching the gospel in Philippi, left Luke there (where the "we" passage ends; see "they" in Acts 16:40). Some years later, in the course of the apostle's third missionary endeavor, Paul and Luke met again in Macedonia, presumably in Philippi (Acts 20:3–5), and Luke rejoined the apostle in his travels (the "we" passages resume), remaining with him all the way to Rome (Acts 28:16). Surprisingly, he is not mentioned in Paul's letter to the Philippians, written toward the end of Paul's first detention in Rome. It is probable Luke was away on some mission. We find him alongside Paul again during the apostle's second Roman detention (2 Timothy 4:11). Obviously Paul was indebted to Luke and had great affection for him, which is why he refers to him as "the beloved physician."

Demas is mentioned along with Luke as conveying greetings to the Colossians. Once again we may assume the church in Colossae either had met or had heard about these two men. "The beloved physician greets you, and Demas." Demas is mentioned only thrice in the New Testament. In Philemon v. 24, he is described, with Luke, as Paul's fellow-worker. However, something happened, and during Paul's second detention in Rome, the apostle wrote, "Demas, in love with this present world, has deserted me and gone to Thessalonica" (2 Timothy 4:10). The circumstances of this desertion are unknown.

Paul had not met the brethren in Laodicea (Colossians 2:1). But he heard of them and they of him, so he wrote, "Greet the brothers in Laodicea, and Nympha and those of the church in her house." Nympha is mentioned only here in the New Testament. She must have been a woman of means if she was able to host a church in her home, although we have no idea of the size of the church in the city. Regular-sized houses in the Roman period could have been able to host no more than a handful. By the time John penned the book of Revelation, the church there would have been quite large.

It is also possible that Paul is referring, not to Nympha (a female) but to Nymphas (a male). However, the feminine is more likely because, in Greek mythology, Nymphe was one of the twelve Horae, the Greek goddesses of the seasons, sometimes a goddess of a lower degree who dwelt in rocks and springs or forests and were beneficent to mankind. A marriageable young woman was also said to be a nymph. Women played a larger role in the early church than some translators and commentators are willing to acknowledge.

In conclusion Paul writes, "And whenever this letter is read to you, see that it is also read in the church of the Laodiceans, so that you also read the letter to those in Laodicea." The churches in the valley naturally maintained a close relationship due not only to their geographical proximity but also to the fact that they seem to have been founded by Epaphras. The letter to the Laodiceans mentioned here cannot be identified with certainty. There are reasons to believe the letter known to us as the letter to the Ephesians was actually a circular letter sent to the three churches, and that the copy to Ephesus was the only copy preserved. Any good introduction to that letter will provide the reader with the argument.

He then adds, "And tell Archippus, 'take care of the service which you have received from the Lord, so you carry it out.'" Like others in this list,

Archippus is mentioned only here and in the letter to Philemon, where Paul called him his fellow-soldier. We know next to nothing of the man and nothing about the nature of the commission to which Paul makes reference. The principle, however, is clear: duties are to be fulfilled, not shirked or neglected. Archippus seems to have belonged in some way to Philemon's household and, since he is mentioned after Philemon and Apphia, thought to have been Philemon's wife; it is probable that Archippus was their son (Philemon v. 2).

Archippus apparently began well. It was now his duty to end well. Good endings are far less common than good beginnings. Is that true of you? Of me? Are we short-winded, impatient, incapable of persevering? Or do we have the reputation of those who, having put their hand to the plough, refuse to look back?

Paul signs off with a signature from his own hand, a final brief request and a salutation: "Greetings in my handwriting, from Paul. Remember my captivity. Grace be with you." It is common but mistaken to think of Paul bent over a papyrus or a writing tablet, carefully devising his letters, erasing and rewriting as he sought the right phrase to express what the Spirit of God was leading him to say. Not so. Paul engaged an amanuensis, a trained professional, something close to a modern secretary, who had the skills and was acquainted with the conventions of the day (a scribe copied, an amanuensis composed). Only the final signature was Paul's (compare Galatians 6:11; 1 Corinthians 16:21). In the letter to the Romans, the amanuensis actually introduces himself ("I Tertius, who wrote this letter, greets you in the Lord" [Romans 16:22]).

In the Roman era, most letters were written on papyrus by means of a reed pen whose point was shaped much like that of a modern fountain pen but requiring skilled, constant sharpening. The ink was generally made of soot mixed with resin to provide permanence and diluted with water to render the ink useable. Writing on papyrus was no easy matter, and the materials for doing so were not in common usage. What is more, the average home (or prison) did not normally hold a stock for letter writing.

Paul would provide the amanuensis with the tone and gist of what he wanted to say. The amanuensis would then compose the letter and submit it to Paul for his approval or correction. If necessary, alterations would be introduced until the apostle was satisfied that the letter expressed what he wanted it to say in the way he wanted to say it. The Spirit of God controlled the whole of this process.

Paul's last two sentences express his own sense of need and summarize the message of his letter: grace is all that counts. Human effort is vacuous and achieves nothing of true spiritual value. Everything a Christian has is by grace, and grace is to be found in Christ alone.

LET'S SUMMARIZE

- Paul recognized his duty to give account of his labors to others. We too should always endeavor to be open to scrutiny, especially if we are involved in the work of the Lord.

- Paul respected those with whom he labored. He was affectionate toward them and did not hesitate to speak well of them. He gave not a thought to the possibility that doing so might detract from his own reputation. Although he had high standards, he knew how to forgive and cultivate others. These are important lessons for all who exercise any kind of leadership in the family, the church, or society.

- Mark was also a man of principle, but he loved the truth and maintained a humility that enabled him to learn and to admit he was wrong when necessary.

- Paul was as human as any of us. He sensed pain and longed for understanding. We should not think of those who lead us as if they are above human sensitivities. We should support them, encourage them, and pray for them.

- God's will is that He would be glorified in Christ through the church. It is for this goal we too should strive.

- We should beware of Demas's example: none of us is secure from sin unless God preserves us. So we should be alert, quick to pray, and firm in the rejection of temptation.

- We thank God for the women among us.

LET'S PRAY

You have chosen to show Your glory

by means of weak and sinful people

and to glorify Yourself in Christ through the church.

May we too love others,

nurture and encourage them,

support them when they fail,

and forgive them when they sin against us.

Move in our hearts, Lord,

to follow Paul's example as he followed Christ's

and to love liberally,

to serve sacrificially,

and to pray earnestly,

not trusting in ourselves but in Your grace.

Protect us from the pride of our hearts

and draw us ever closer to Yourself,

so that we might do Your will

to the praise of the glory of Your grace,

through Jesus Christ our Lord, amen.

QUESTIONS FOR DISCUSSION AND STUDY

1. Choose two of the individuals named in this passage and learn from the Scriptures all you can. Try to draw an outline of their spiritual and moral character (be careful to base your views on Scripture). What can you learn from these two for your own life?

2. Make a list of ways you can encourage scrutiny of your life and accountability in relation to others.

3. In what ways does Paul exemplify the principles he taught in this letter? Summarize the lessons you have derived from this under two columns—principles and practice—with three headings for each.

Summary

To Whom the Glory?

Every word in this letter, even the apostle's commendations in the opening statements, was designed to correct an error Paul identified among the Colossians. He was not trying to pander to his readers' vanity in the hope of gaining a listening ear; he had something important to say. Chapter 1 is replete with indirect references to a truth Paul brought out in the course of his letter and that the Colossians were inclined to forget: there are no grounds for spiritual elitism.

All the Colossians were and had was a gift of grace through Christ from God. No honor for spiritual achievement could be attributed to them; it was all the product of Christ's glorious person and His sufficient work on their behalf. God was to be thanked for everything. Even the Colossians' faith and love for others were gifts (1:1–5), as were their hope and security (1:5). Nothing was the reward of a well-practiced spirituality.

The catalogue of God's gifts to the Colossians continues, with Paul employing terminology borrowed from the false teaching being promulgated in Colossae: the Father "delivered us from the domain of darkness" (1:13)—a phrase the false teachers in Colossae used to describe the spiritual state of the unenlightened. Paul would have the Colossians remember that enlightenment was a gift of grace, not the reward of virtue.

The kingdom to which the Colossian Christians were transferred was the "kingdom of [God's] beloved Son" (1:13). No spiritual patron, no angel, none but the Son is honored there. In the Son, the Colossians had obtained redemption, the forgiveness of sins (1:14). Christ—not a priest or a spiritually endowed individual—is the "head of the church" and its assurance of resurrection (1:18). None— "on earth or in heaven" (1:20)— are reconciled to God, but through Him (1:21–22).

Commending the Colossians for their inclusive love, Paul also credited that love to the Spirit of God (1:8). Everything commendable about the Colossians was attributed to God: Paul was an apostle by the will of God. The Colossians were consecrated because they had been chosen by God. Strength, knowledge, and understanding come only as the fruit of the workings of God (1:11).

Men contribute nothing to their salvation, nor can they contribute anything to the security of their salvation; it is all of God. These are truths Christians should gladly embrace because they are the grounds of their security. There is a danger that we will deny such truths by our attitude toward those whose understanding or practice of the Christian Faith differs from our own or by thinking that, in some way, we contributed to our salvation—as if sanctification is not an aspect of the fruit of Christ's saving work and of the Spirit's gracious application.

Satan subtly seeks to transform even the recognition of worthlessness into grounds for pride. How humble have we been about God's gifts to us? That is a major question the letter to the Colossians forces upon us.

Paul's concern over the Colossians' error was due to his objection to anything that tended to obscure Christ's glory, as does any sense of elitism or reliance on human endeavor. Opposing such was Paul's consuming passion. It should be ours. Jesus is everything: our salvation, our sanctification, and the sum of our hope. All we have from God, we have by Jesus' virtues. All God will ever give us, do for us, or accomplish in us is the fruit of Jesus' death and resurrection. The life that we now live, and that we will live in eternity, is by the virtue of the Son of God, who loved us and gave Himself for us.

For that reason, Paul labored in this letter to point his readers to Christ's all-sufficiency. He was convinced that, in the blaze of Christ's glory, the Colossian error would be seen as the lie it was. Who can improve on the light of the sun? Who can add to what Jesus has accomplished?

Nothing Beyond Christ

Christians are now "in the kingdom of His beloved Son," where the Son alone is to have glory. The last times are upon us, and the kingdom to be is the kingdom that now is. The Colossians had been encouraged by some to believe that there was another stage, beyond salvation, an experience of enlightenment that would lift them to a higher plane of spirituality. Forgiveness of sins was one thing, but redemption from darkness was another.

In response, in 1:13, Paul used the terms employed by the teachers of purported truth, insisting that all who are forgiven also partake of redemption in its fullest sense. There is no two-stage salvation—first forgiveness, then enlightenment or spiritual endowment. The Spirit does not add to what Jesus has accomplished or bring Christians a single step further in terms of spirituality. All is to be found in Christ, is contingent upon Him, and flows from His glorious person. Jesus is either both Lord and Savior, or He is neither. When a person is regenerated, he receives full redemption. Systems that deny this truth are man-made and therefore false. They obscure the glory of Christ by presuming to add to His accomplishments, diluting the gospel, and ultimately making man his own savior.

No One Beyond Christ

Paul went on to speak of the glories of Christ. His motive was pastoral. He was not engaged in a theoretical discussion of abstract metaphysics but of the essence of the Christian life and of Christian congregational life. He was not asking how many angels can dance on the head of a pin but laboring for the spiritual health of the people of God. He was engaged in a struggle for the glory of his Savior and for the church as a visible expression of the gospel of God's grace.

The Colossians were in danger of being duped into believing they could add to the achievements of Christ by legalistic customs, by the adoption of spiritual patrons, and by mystical experiences. "No!" said Paul. The Son is the very "fullness" (1:19; 2:9), the "image of the invisible God" (1:15). You cannot get beyond Jesus if you wish to know God. Beyond Him is utter darkness, a vacuum of nothingness.

True, there are lesser sources of information: Paul did not hesitate to say in Romans 1 that creation speaks of God. But God's most exact and exhausting representation is to be had nowhere but in His Son. For that reason, the worship of angels (2:18), those spiritual patrons the Colossians were invited to adopt on their way to God, were of no value. Men are too vile to have access to the Most High and Spiritual One. But there is nothing they can do to change that; it was done by Christ. Access is by grace, not through demonstrations of self-abasement or the worship of angels.

There is nothing man can do to gain access to God. No forgoing of earthly enjoyments, no denying of worldly lusts will do. Man cannot find God by escaping the world. Jesus, the true image of God, made everything that exists and sustains an ongoing relation to it. The material world was considered by the Colossian heretics too gross, too unclean to have anything to do with Ultimate Divinity. True spirituality was perceived by them to be obtainable by abstaining from the world: "Don't touch, don't handle, don't eat." Such an attitude, rather than contributing to an advanced spirituality, distanced the Colossians from it because it obscured the glory of God's grace through His Son. The belief that man could do something in an effort to gain spiritual achievements promoted a sense of human accomplishment that is far removed from biblical spirituality. It is a form of self-salvation that denies the gospel by implication, regardless of how much it might insist on grace.

Legalism and the World

The "fullness", of which the Colossians had been taught to understand as that which separated them from the Ultimate and that sphere into which they must ascend to achieve the Ultimate, is not a series of emanations and patron angels. It is in Christ, in whom it pleased the Father that all fullness should dwell, and Christians "are complete in Him" (2:10). No more is needed.

Salvation is all of one piece: it is of grace. It is in Christ. It is complete in Him, and all the Colossians had to do to experience it was focus on Christ and to set their minds on things above, where Christ is seated at the right hand of God, rather than be taken up with earthly matters such as those that occupy the minds of legalists. Is it not true that the subject that most occupies the minds of those who wish to lose weight is the food they must not eat? Is it not true that those most taken up with the need to breathe are those who for any reason cannot do so? The proper course was neither in denying their flesh nor in yielding to it but in setting their minds on Jesus.

The Colossians were told Christ was too spiritual to have been God become man, that He disavowed anything that had to do with "the flesh." However much it might shake the Colossians' sensitivities, Paul insisted that the divine Fullness dwelt in Christ bodily. Christ embraced and redeemed the world by becoming part of it. The divine fullness, the Son, the very image of God, is so closely related to the physical that He took to Himself what Paul describes as a "fleshly body" (1:22).

To counter the false view, Paul insisted on describing Jesus as having come in a "fleshly body": He was so human as to bleed and die (1:20, 22). "The fullness of deity dwells in Him in bodily form" (2:9). He did not escape the earthly to be spiritual or avoid contact with it. He took it up with no reduction of His spirituality—and so must all Christians. A hearty love of the world in Christ is no less necessary than a rejection of it when it denies or seeks to supplant Him. God has provided for us bountifully and for our holy enjoyment. We evidence our spirituality when we enjoy His gifts without becoming addicted to them or valuing them above the Giver.

The false teachers insisted on the lack of spirituality of the visible world, but the gospel has a positive view of the world. It reminds us that God created it and declared it good; that it was made for pleasure and enjoyment; that it is where God is to be loved and honored. Material blessing is a gift from God. Spirituality does not have to do with abstinence from pleasure, except sinful pleasure.

Legalism obscures the glory of Christ for two main reasons: it denies His glory as Lord of creation, and it proceeds on the false assumption that man can escape the world and thereby achieve a heightened form of spirituality. True spirituality is, among other things, an experience of human community and substantial, intellectual knowledge, of "being linked together by love and leading to all the riches that belong to a full assurance of understanding, leading in turn to full knowledge of God's mystery—Christ—in whom are hidden all the treasures of wisdom and knowledge" (2:2-4).

It has to do with society, with life, with instruction that leads to proper comprehensions (2:7), not with mystical experiences; with gratitude for what has been done for us, not with a sense of self-satisfaction because we've managed to do something. It has to do with Jews and Gentiles, slaves and freemen, and women and men worshipping God together. It is by grace in Christ.

Grace and Works

This leads us to one of the more engaging aspects of truth: the tension it creates. Truth is full of antinomies, realities that seem to conflict with one another but, in fact, combine to make up the totality of what is. That totality is too large, too complex, and too rich for human comprehension, and so we are forced to think in terms of antinomies. Law and grace is one such tension, of which grace and works is a practical aspect.

True, the Colossians had received much by grace. What they received remained theirs by that same grace. But there was no room for indolence. "He who endures to the end shall be saved" is the converse of the truth that they were "kept by the power of God for a salvation that is ready to be revealed." Nothing is to be considered secure until fully enjoyed. As the writer to the Hebrews said, "We have become [past tense] partakers of Christ if [conditional] we hold fast [present continuous] the beginning of our assurance firm until the end" (Hebrews 3:14). Jesus, Paul, and the writer to the Hebrews were not of the opinion that we obtain salvation by virtue of our faith nor that we preserve our salvation on the grounds of faithful obedience and continued faith. But they knew and taught that grace is never to be viewed as an opportunity for spiritual or moral laxity. Grace puts us to work.

Such a truth is what grace uses to move men to exert themselves more strenuously and to sacrifice with more abandon than if they had to earn salvation by works. The test of their saving faith is their endurance. They have been reconciled *if*: "if indeed you continue in the Faith ... not moved away from the hope of the gospel" (1:22–23).

Grace and Unity

The Colossians were to set aside the patterns of their former sinful behavior: in a society where class was all important, they were called upon to relate to one another—slaves and masters, husbands and wives, parents and children, Jews and Gentiles—with mutual respect and without regard for the social norms that divided mankind (3:5–4:1). No one was to be above another; Christ was above them all, and His glory was not to be obscured by undue self-appreciation, social sectarianism, or religious arrogance. The fact that Christians differ is not as important as how they relate to one another in the face of their differences. Their divisions are an insult to the glory of Christ. His splendor should cause their differences to fade into relative unimportance.

Paul called the Colossians "consecrated ones and faithful brethren" (1:2), referring in one breath both to their relation to God and to one another because one cannot be faithful without being consecrated by an empowering act of God, and one cannot be consecrated without being faithful. Consecrated ones are those who have been called by God into a community of God's own making. As such, the Colossians had duties toward one another no amount of spiritual gifting could obviate.

We also know God's grace. We too are called into that community and bear a responsibility toward all who belong to it. Some are likeable, and some are not; some are Lutherans and some are Baptists or Presbyterians. Some are Pentecostal and some are Charismatic. We speak different languages, come from different cultures, understand different kinds of music, and have different social expectations. But, like the Colossians, we should be characterized by a generous love to all the consecrated ones (1:4), and that love should be translated into shared congregational life because that is the framework God ordained and into which He has called all members of the community He is creating. That and no other. In its stead, the present division of the church of Christ is an abomination, a denial of the principle of salvation by grace, and a major stumbling block to a coherent witness to the world.

Not Yet Arrived

Theories of spiritual achievement encourage a sense of superiority, the kind Paul labored in this letter to deny. However commendable the Colossians' achievements might have been, Paul spurred them to aspire for more by describing his prayers for them (1:9ff). They had not yet reached the perfection purchased by Christ—the fullness, as some preferred to call it. They did not "have it all." They were still short of the basic foundation stones for a proper Christian life, such as "knowledge of God's will and spiritual wisdom and understanding" (1:9). Their measure of knowledge needed to become motivation to live "in a manner worthy of the Lord" that they might "please Him in all respects" and increase in their "knowledge of God" (1:10).

Knowing is simply not enough—and the Colossians certainly did not know all that could be known. Do we? Doing is important, and the Colossians certainly didn't do enough. Do we? Doing is a condition for fuller knowing. What will it us profit if we know all mysteries and have all knowledge, yet do not practice what we know by loving our brethren? What kind of knowledge can we have when our theory is not followed by practice? What kind of love do we exercise if we consider ourselves better than fellow Christians because we believe we're more enlightened, and when our professed acknowledgements of Christian unity are so often limited to verbal assertions and have little practical effect?

Doing is not only necessary for knowledge, it leads to conduct that pleases God because it is characterized by a patient, joyful consistency that delights to praise Him for qualifying us "to share in the inheritance of the consecrated ones in light" (1:12) and recognizes the essential one-ness of all members in the body of Christ. In other words, true Christian spirituality is humble: it attributes nothing to itself. It dares not arrogate to itself a worth that comes from God by grace alone. That is why it en-tertains a love "for all the consecrated ones" (1:4), made to be such by the virtues of Christ. The glory of that grace is revealed when men who differ love one another. It is obscured when practical expressions of love are made conditional upon full agreement.

We abjure legalism. But are we not sometimes in danger of insisting upon behavioral shibboleths that have a flimsy scriptural basis? Are not many of our legalisms the product of insecurity and an inability to trust Christ to accomplish His will in our life or that of others? Shouldn't we occupy our minds more "on the things above, where Christ is seated at the right hand of God rather than on the things that are on the earth"? Is it possible we are guilty of a "touch not, taste not, handle not" attitude instead of exulting in the glories of Christ?

An area in which the glory of Christ is frequently obscured is the manner in which Christians relate to one another. No quarrel is more divisive than a religious quarrel. The extent to which we understand and believe the doctrines of the gospel is often contrary to the way we treat fellow Christians, especially those who do not share our particular con-victions. I confess with shame that I have often fallen short in this re-spect myself. I gladly admit that I have learned much from brethren with whom I firmly disagree. It is a truth I cannot deny: grace requires of me to affirm my unity with those whose view of grace is what I consider to be faulty, and I must beware of Satan's effort to subvert my views of grace by transforming them into grounds for arrogance and pride.

May God help me, and you, and all His church. No doubt, we need that help.

You are welcome to write me at bmaoz@themaozweb.com

Regular postings may be found on my website
(www.themaozweb.com),
my Facebook and LinkedIn pages, and through Twitter.

A monthly newsletter is available for the asking
at the above e-mail address.

If you've benefited from this book, help us promote its distribution by writing a review on Amazon's and Barnes & Noble's pages and on any Christian readers' blog with which you are acquainted.

Thank you for this help.

CPSIA information can be obtained
at www.ICGtesting.com
Printed in the USA
BVHW042308051222
653543BV00003B/24

9 781943 539109